Preference Laws
for Syllable Structure

Theo Vennemann

# Preference Laws
# for Syllable Structure

and the Explanation
of Sound Change

With Special Reference to German,
Germanic, Italian, and Latin

1988
Mouton de Gruyter
Berlin · New York · Amsterdam

*Theo Vennemann genannt Nierfeld*
Chair of Germanic and Theoretical Linguistics
University of Munich

Mouton de Gruyter (formerly Mouton, The Hague)
is a Division of Walter de Gruyter & Co., Berlin.

Library of Congress Cataloging-in-Publication Data

**Vennemann, Theo.**
  Preference laws for syllable structure and the
explanation of sound change.

  Bibliography: p.
  Includes index.
1. Grammar, Comparative and general-Syllable.
2. Grammar, Comparative and general-Phonology.
3. Linguistic change. I. Title.
P236.V46   1988        414        87-31509
ISBN 0-89925411-X (alk. paper)

CIP-Titelaufnahme der Deutschen Bibliothek

**Vennemann, Theo:**
Preference laws for syllable structure and the explanation of
sound change/Theo Vennemann. – Berlin; New York;
Amsterdam: Mouton de Gruyter, 1988
  ISBN 3-11-011375-9

Printed on acid free paper.

Typesetting and Printing: Tutte Druckerei GmbH, Passau-Salzweg. –
Binding: Lüderitz & Bauer, Berlin. – Printed in Germany.

For
*Terence H. Wilbur,*
Germanist, Bascologist, linguist
at UCLA,
homme savant and academician,
my Doktorvater,
a wise and kindly man

# Preface

This booklet contains the text, augmented mainly by explanatory notes and an index, of a lecture presented at the University of California, Berkeley, on April 22, 1985. I would like to thank the Department of German, especially Professors Irmengard Rauch, Herbert Penzl, and Thomas Shannon, for their invitation and their hospitality on and around the Berkeley Campus.

I am also grateful to Professors Walburga von Raffler Engel and Alice C. Harris for discussing some of the ideas presented in this lecture during a very pleasant stay at Vanderbilt University in Nashville, Tennessee, April 15–18, 1985.

The first incentive to bring together my ideas on preferred syllable structure and on syllable structure change and to illustrate them with Germanic and Italian examples came with an invitation from Professor Alberto Mioni to discuss this as well as other work with him, his colleagues, and his students at the University of Padua. I will always be grateful for those beautiful, challenging early spring days of 1984 and 1985 which I had the good fortune of spending in the venerable University of Padua, founded 1222, and its 18th century Maldura Palace.

Thanks go to Professor Sang-Oak Lee of Seoul National University for affording the manuscript of my lecture some initial, working paper style distribution in *Papers in Phonology and Morphology III*, ed. by the Phonology Workshop of the Linguistic Society of Korea,

Seoul (Pan Korea Book Corporation), 1985, and for pointing out some errors in that manuscript.

Thanks are due, once again, to Tom Shannon who, in a long discussion between Benicia and Berkeley on April 17, 1986, and by applying and improving the Preference Laws framework in some of his own publications, has persuaded me to present this lecture to a wider audience.

Last but not least, I wish to thank the Stiftung Volkswagenwerk for granting me an Akademie-Stipendium for two semesters, enabling me to find the time to arrange this text for publication.

D-8901 Ried, May 1986                     Theo Vennemann

# Contents

# Introduction

This lecture deals with syllable structure, in particular with changes in syllable structure. It presents preference laws for syllable structure. These laws specify the preferred syllabic patterns of natural languages as well as determine the direction of syllable structure change.

## The Concept of Preference Laws

My conception of preference laws[1] differs from most approaches to linguistic naturalness by characterizing linguistic structure not as good or bad (natural or unnatural, unmarked or marked), but as better or worse. It develops a graded concept of linguistic quality relative to a given parameter.[2] The parameters in this lecture are aspects of syllable structure. It is important to keep this in mind, because what is better relative to one parameter or set of parameters may be worse relative to others. Nothing in the world is good or bad *an sich*. The basic concept of the theory outlined here is 'X is the more preferred in terms of (a given parameter of) syllable structure, the more Y', where X is a phonological pattern and Y a gradable property of X. But the presentation of the laws will be very informal in this lecture.

The correctness of a preference law can be checked as follows. Every change in a language system is a local improvement, i.e. an improvement relative to a certain pa-

1

rameter. For instance, every syllable structure change is an improvement of syllable structure as defined by some preference law for syllable structure. If a change worsens syllable structure, it is not a syllable structure change, by which I mean a change motivated by syllable structure, but a change on some other parameter which merely happens also to affect syllable structure. This is true, e.g., of diphthongizations, which are paradigmatically rather than syntagmatically motivated changes, and of syncope and apocope, which are manifestations of the preference for briefness. Both diphthongizations and copations by necessity change the syllable structure of the affected items or even of the language system, and indeed always worsen it.[3] But they evidently are not syllable structure changes. Since every change is an improvement, a change on a given parameter is motivated by the inherent low degree of linguistic quality of the affected structures relative to that parameter. Even though in principle improvement could start anywhere, with the best structures as well as with the worst or somewhere in the middle, one might venture the hypothesis that in fact remedial measures will not be applied to better structures as long as there are worse ones on the same parameter.

(1)    **Diachronic Maxim:** Linguistic change on a given parameter does not affect a language structure as long as there exist structures in the language system that are less preferred in terms of the relevant preference law.

In other words, linguistic change on a given parameter attacks the worst structures first. I am convinced that this hypothesis is correct, and I can therefore use linguistic change as a testing ground for my preference laws.

Every language system represents a stage in a history

of change. Since change is governed by the Diachronic Maxim, one will expect language systems in general not to contain language structures on a given parameter in the absence of structures constructible with the means of the system which are more preferred on the same parameter.

(2) **Synchronic Maxim:** A language system will in general not contain a structure on a given parameter without containing those structures constructible with the means of the system that are more preferred in terms of the relevant preference law.

Since any linguistic change eliminates a continuous range of structures of relatively low quality from a parameter, the result will be a continuous range of structures of relatively high quality on that parameter.[4]

(3)

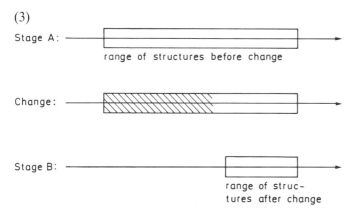

Stage A:

range of structures before change

Change:

Stage B:

range of struc-
tures after change

Structures arranged on a parameter in the order of increasing preference

This is indeed the normal situation. However, changes run along many parameters, and they may incidentally shoot holes in parameters that are not theirs, or place structures on parameters that combine with the pre-existing structures to form discontinuous ranges. Ranges of structures may also contain "natural gaps", owing to some special combinatory constraint. Finally, borrowing may create discontinuous ranges. Nevertheless, the normal situation occurs with sufficient frequency to suggest the use of language systems as another testing ground for preference laws.

The preference laws are universals. They are theorems of a general theory of the human communicative capacity. In particular, the preference laws for syllable structure have their basis in the human productive and perceptive phonetic endowment. They, as well as their natural gaps, would be derivable – and thus explained – in a sufficiently rich phonetic theory. Since I am not a phonetician, I will make no attempt to explain my preference laws for syllable structure.

The assumed universality of the preference laws does not preclude that within limits users of a language system may develop their own concept of system-specific normalcy, which need not coincide with maximal universal preference.[5] This is so precisely because language systems are products of human history and are thus cultural rather than natural entities. Nevertheless, all natural language systems only exist by virtue of the fact that they have been induced by human beings approaching the task with nothing but a natural endowment. It is this fact which accounts for the great amount of uniformity among language systems. Without it there could be no universal preference laws but only statements of language-specific normalcy.

# Basic Concepts of Syllabic Phonology

I will make a few simple assumptions about the structure of syllables, and even though the very conception of a syllabic patterning in natural language systems may be questioned,[6] I will make no effort to defend them here. For the present discussion I will assume '(possible) **syllable**' and '(possible) **word**' to be primitive concepts.

The (possible) syllables of a language system are specified by a function $\sigma$ which assigns each syllable its phonologically relevant properties. There are two sorts of properties: **basic properties** and **prosodic properties**. Thus $\sigma$ is actually the conjunct of two functions, BA and $\pi$, such that BA assigns each syllable its basic properties, and $\pi$ its prosodic properties.[7] The basic function assigns each syllable a sequence of speech sounds, the **basis** of the syllable.[8] The prosodic function $\pi$ is the conjunct of several functions – possibly empty in part – which assign each syllable its **nuclear**, **moric**, **tonal**, and **cut** (or **ballistic**) **properties**[9] as well as others, e.g. the presence or absence of the stød in Danish. Of these, the nucleus function NU, which characterizes one of the speech sound occurrences in the basis of the syllable as the designated element of the syllable, its **nucleus**, is never empty.[10] For many – I believe, most – language systems the values of this function are entirely predictable. For some languages, however, this particular prosody is contrastive,[11] which means that it has to be provided for in a general phonological theory.

Given that the basis BA and the nucleus NU are thus specified for each syllable, further functions become definable: HE, which assigns each syllable that part of its basis which precedes its nucleus, its **head**; CO, which assigns each syllable that part of its basis which follows its nucleus, its **coda**; BO, which assigns each syllable the union of its head and nucleus, its **body**; and RY, which assigns each syllable the union of its nucleus and its coda, its **rhyme**; and SH, which assigns each syllable the union of its head and its coda, its **shell**.[12] A cover term for the heads and codas of syllables is **margin**. A syllable with an empty margin is called **naked** or **open**, depending on whether its body or rhyme is concerned: it is naked if its head is empty, and it is open if its coda is empty; otherwise the syllable is called **covered** or **closed**, respectively.[13] An open syllable with a short nucleus is **light**; all others are **heavy**.[14] Light syllables count one mora; in heavy syllables length adds one mora, and so does every additional rhyme speech sound. If length is not represented as a prosody but as an additional identical speech sound, the number of moras of a syllable is simply the cardinality of its rhyme.[15] The most common phonologically relevant distinction in language systems is that between one-mora syllables and more-than-one-mora syllables. It is easy to see that this is the same distinction as that between light and heavy syllables.

The expressions **onset** and **offset** are employed here in their most ordinary usage, viz. for the first and final speech sound occurrence of a given sequence, especially of a syllable head or coda, respectively. The onset and offset of a higher-order unit will simply be that of the relevant sequence of speech sounds; thus, the onset of a syllable will be that of its head (= that of its basis), its offset that of its coda (= that of its basis).[16] The **slope** of a margin is the margin minus its onset or offset, depending on whether the margin is a head or a coda, respectively. (This definition has to be restricted to cores, see pp. 9–10.)

The (possible) words of a language system are specified by a function $\lambda$ which assigns each word its system-relevant properties. There are two sorts of properties: **phonological properties**, assigned by a function $\varphi$, and **conceptual properties**, viz. the syntactic, semantic, and pragmatic use properties, assigned by a function $c$, which is of no interest in the present context.[17]

There are two sorts of phonological properties of words, **foundation properties**, assigned by a function FO, and **prosodic properties**, assigned by a function $\Pi$. The foundation function FO assigns each word a finite sequence of syllables, its **foundation**. The word prosody function $\Pi$ is the conjunct of several functions – possibly empty in part – which assign each word its **tonal properties** (insofar as these are not inherent properties of the individual syllables in its foundation), its **accentual properties** (e.g. the position of that syllable in the foundation which receives the sentence accent), **harmonic properties**, and possibly others.[18]

Given two adjacent syllables – within the foundation of a single word or across a word boundary – we can define the **contact** of this pair of syllables as that sequence of speech sounds which consists of the offset of the first syllable and the onset of the second syllable, in that order. Thus, if the first syllable has the basis /ar/, and the second /ma/, their syllable contact would be /rm/; with /a/ and /ra/, it would be /ar/. To stress the fact that the speech sounds of a syllable contact occur before and after a "syllable boundary", I may write /r.m/, /a.r/ or /r$^\$$m/, /a$^\$$r/.[19] With A and B as variables for speech sounds, A.B and A$^\$$B would thus be informal notations for a syllable contact.

From the foundation of a given word we may derive its **basis** BA (I deliberately use the same expression as for syllables) as the concatenation of the bases of all the syllables in the foundation. So, if a word $\Lambda_1$ has the foundation $\langle \Sigma_1, \Sigma_2 \rangle$ such that BA$(\Sigma_1)$ = /ar/ and BA$(\Sigma_2)$ = /ma/, this function would derive /arma/ as the basis of $\Lambda_1$.[20]

Given a word $\Lambda$, we may also view its phonological form $\varphi(\Lambda)$ as a pair consisting of the basis of $\Lambda$ and the

**composite prosody** (or simply: the **prosody**) of $\Lambda$. The composite prosody of $\Lambda$ would comprise the syllable structure properties inherent in its foundation, the prosodic properties inherent in the syllables of its foundation, and its word-prosodic properties in the narrower sense of $\Pi(\Lambda)$. Viewed in this way, the fact that the basis /arma/ of $\Lambda_1$ is divided by a syllable boundary as /ar.ma/ becomes part of the composite prosody of $\Lambda_1$, even though it is derived from its foundation $FO(\Lambda_1)$ rather than from its word prosody $\Pi(\Lambda_1)$. The concept of a composite prosody allows us furthermore to speak about such derivative phenomena as ambisyllabicity and internal tonal or accentual sandhi in a natural way. For example, **ambisyllabicity** would derive from the juxtaposition of an abruptly cut syllable[21] and a covered syllable in this order, provided that the contact of this pair of syllables fulfills certain requirements pertaining to the relative Consonantal Strength of its elements (Consonantal Strength in the sense to be discussed directly); the abruptly cut syllable attracts the onset of the covered syllable to its own basis so as to emphasize its abruptly cut or "arrested" quality. Thus, in standard varieties of English the first syllable of *citric* (basis /sɪ/) is abruptly cut; it attracts the onset of the second syllable (basis /trək/) to its own basis, making this occurrence of /t/ ambisyllabic.

The speech sounds of a language system have **phonetic correlates**, which may differ according to their syntagmatic and prosodic contexts. These correlates may be projected on a phonetic parameter of degree of deviation from unimpeded (voiced) air flow, called **Universal Consonantal Strength**. This projection induces an ordering among the correlates. If we decide to associate with each speech sound one of its correlates as its **principal correlate** (the terminology is to be reminiscent of the idea of the principal allophone of a phoneme) and to consider only the order induced among the principal correlates by Universal Consonantal Strength, then we may consider the speech sounds themselves ordered by Strength, viz. via their principal correlates. Even though there may exist considerable differences among language systems – e.g., the principal correlate of a speech sound transcribed as /r/ may be a very weak impediment to (voiced) air flow in normal utterances for one language system but a fairly strong one in another – in general the order induced on the speech sounds is as in (4).

(4) 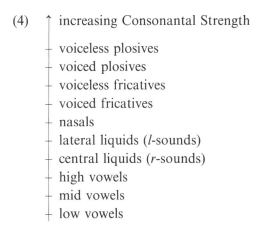 increasing Consonantal Strength

voiceless plosives
voiced plosives
voiceless fricatives
voiced fricatives
nasals
lateral liquids (*l*-sounds)
central liquids (*r*-sounds)
high vowels
mid vowels
low vowels

The concept of Consonantal Strength allows us to define the concept of **monotonicity** for heads, bodies, codas, rhymes, and syllables. Heads and bodies are called **weakly monotonic** if no rise, and codas and rhymes, if no fall of Consonantal Strength occurs in them. Heads, bodies, codas, and rhymes are called **strongly monotonic** if they are weakly monotonic and do not contain sound occurrences of equal Strength.[22] A syllable is called **weakly (strongly) monotonic** if both its body and its rhyme are weakly (strongly) monotonic.[23] A strongly monotonic syllable is called a **core syllable**.[24] The largest portion of a syllable basis that could be the basis of a core syllable is called the **core** of the syllable. To illustrate, the core of the syllable of English *skill* is /kɪl/, because the syllable of *kill* is a core syllable and no larger portion of /skɪl/ could be the basis of a core syllable.[25] Those largest portions of syllable bases that are outside the core are the syllables' **appendices**. Thus, the syllable of the English word *sprints* has the **prependix** /s/ and the **suppendix** [7]/s/; and the syllable of the Standard German word *Herbsts* 'autumn (gen.)' with the basis /hɛrpsts/ has the suppendix [5]/sts/. If a notation is needed, appendices and cores may be separated in phonological representations by a thin vertical stroke, e.g. /s|prɪnt|s/, /hɛrp|sts/. Appendices induce the formation of one or several **quasi-syllables** (*Nebensilben* in Sievers 1901: § 543) with their own **quasi-nuclei** (marked " ꞁ " on the analogy of " ι " for nuclei), **quasi-margins**, etc.; the quasi-syllable boundary may be indicated by a comma (on the analogy of the period for syllable boundaries), e.g. [s,prɪnt], [s,prɪn,ts], [hɛr,ps,ts].

# The Preference Laws

Next I turn to a formulation and justification of the most prominent preference laws for syllable structure. The laws to be discussed are those in (5).

(5)   A. Preference laws for individual syllables
          1. The Head Law (6)
          2. The Coda Law (25)
          3. The Nucleus Law (42)

     B. Preference laws for sequences of syllables
          4. The Weight Law (45)
          5. The Law of Initials (51)
          6. The Law of Finals (54)
          7. The Strength Assimilation Law (58)
          8. The Contact Law (67)

The list of laws as formulated in the course of this discussion is unsatisfactory in a number of respects. First, there are undoubtedly many more laws. Thus, there must be a **Shell Law**, because over and above the preferences for the structure of heads and codas, there exist preferences for their combination within the same syllable. In general, a shell seems to be the more preferred, the less similar the head and (the mirror image of) the coda are. In particular, identical speech sounds flanking the nucleus are disfavored, all the more so the less their Consonantal Strength is. The antipathy increases notably if the identical speech sounds flanking the nucleus are not the only ones within their margins. For English, this aversion has the well-known consequence that it does not have lexical monosyllables of the shape (C)RVR'(C'), where R and R' are identical resonants (nasals, liquids, or vocalic glides), V is a monophthong, C and C' are consonants, and the parentheses mean that at least one of the two positions is filled. There must further be a **Body Law** and a **Rhyme Law** expressing degrees of preference for combinations of nuclei with heads and codas, respectively. For instance, ongliding and offgliding nuclear speech sounds often impose additional restrictions on the structure of heads and codas – as though the gliding portion of the polyphthong were actually a part of the adjacent margin.[26] There must also be preference laws for the structure of syllables in relation to the **tones** they bear; the fact that many tone (or pitch accent) languages prohibit non-level tones (chromatic accents) on short vowels – or more generally on syllables of less than two voiced moric speech sounds – would be a manifestation of such preferences.

Secondly, the laws to be discussed are presented without any indication of possible specific restrictions on the combination of individual (groups of) sounds, such as denti-alveolar plosives and lateral liquids (in this order).[27]

Thirdly, the laws as formulated contain a certain amount of redundancy. For instance, as will be seen, it follows from the Coda and Nucleus Laws that a syllable will be the more preferrred, the less the Consonantal Strength of its offset is, and from the Head Law that a syllable will be the more preferred, the greater the Consonantal Strength of its onset is. The laws do not restrict this to syllables in isolation. For syllables in contact, however, the same two points also follow – at least the one for the first and the other for the second of the abutting syllables – from the Contact Law.

I believe that despite all shortcomings, the laws as formulated here are not entirely without value. At least they summarize a significant portion of the results of a century of research on the structure of syllables, especially inasmuch as it relates to a concept of Consonantal Strength, all the way from Eduard Sievers, Otto Jespersen, Ferdinand de Saussure, and Maurice Grammont to W. Sidney Allen, Joan Bybee Hooper, Robert W. Murray, and some of those working within one or the other prosody-oriented framework of transformational grammar. I hope nevertheless that my summarizing and integrating approach, together with the abundant exemplification, may serve as a welcome introduction to the study of syllable structure. Its greatest success would be to provoke the research that is needed to overcome the deficiencies and imprecisions that mar the present formulation.

As for the exemplification, whose real purpose is the justification of the laws, I have chosen my material mainly from the history of two languages, German and Italian, including their dialects,[28] in order to underline the essentially non-idiosyncratic nature of the illustrated changes. But I take the liberty of freely adding examples from other languages for change types that are not – or not as beautifully – represented in the two.

## The Head Law

(6)   **Head Law**
      A syllable head is the more preferred: (a) the closer the number of speech sounds in the head is to one, (b) the greater the Consonantal Strength value of its onset, and (c) the more sharply the Consonantal

Strength drops from the onset toward the Consonantal Strength of the following syllable nucleus.

The number of speech sounds in a syllable head may deviate from one in two directions. It may be less than one,
viz. zero. Part (a) of the law suggests that there will be
changes filling the onset position; and there are indeed.
Northern speakers of German insert glottal stops at the
beginning of naked syllables, especially word-initial and
stressed ones:

(7)   *Ɂalt, Ɂa.Ɂór.ta, cha.Ɂó.tisch, chá.os (cha.Ɂos)*

Italian developed glides out of contiguous vowels, which
after strengthening became regular onset speech sounds.

(8)   (a) *Ge.nu.a*      > *Ge.no.va*
          *Man.tu.a*     > *Man.to.va*
          *Pa.du.a*      > *Pa.do.va*
          *vi.du.a*      > *ve.do.va* 'widow'
          *ma.nu.a.le* > *ma.no.va.le* 'handyman'
          *ru.i.na*      > *ro.vi.na* 'ruin'
          *pac.tu i.re* > *pat.to.vi.re* 'to negotiate'
          *Pau.lo*       > *Pa.o.lo* > $\begin{cases} Pa.vo.lo \\ Pa.go.lo \end{cases}$

      (b) *ma.te.ri.a.le* > *⁺ma.dri.a.le* >
          *ma.dri.ga.le* 'madrigal'
          *An.dre.a* > *An.dre.ia* (Old Tuscan)
          *des.tru.e.re* > *⁺dis.tru.ie.re* >
          *dis.trùg.ge.re* 'destroy'

For heads with more than one speech sound, part (a) of
the Head Law suggests changes reducing their number. In
Pāli (as well as other Middle Indic dialects), all head clus-

14

ters – abundant in Sanskrit – were reduced to one element, usually by deletion, sometimes by anaptyxis; cf. Murray 1982, who follows Geiger 1916 and Grammont 1950.

(9)  (a)  *prajnā* > *paññā*                        'knowledge'
         *krayavikraya* > *kayavikkaya*   'commerce'
         *srotas* > *sota*                        'stream'
         *svapna* > *soppa*                    'sleep'
         *syandana* > *sandana*          'wagon'

     (b)  *ām.ra* > $^+$*am.bra* > *am.ba*  'mango'

     (c)  *tak.ra* > $^+$*tak.kra* > *tak.ka* 'whey'
         *krayavikraya* > $^+$*kra.ya.vik.kra.ya* >
             *ka.ya.vik.ka.ya* 'commerce'
         *svap.na* > $^+$*svap.pna* > *sop.pa* 'sleep'
         *kal.ya* > $^+$*kal.lya* > *kal.la* 'ready'
         *miś.ra* > $^+$*mis.sra* > *mis.sa* 'mixed'
         *aś.va* > $^+$*as.sva* > *as.sa*    'horse'

     (d)  *sneha* > *si.ne.ha*                  'affection'
         *plakṣa* > *pi.lak.khu*             (name of tree)
         *dve* > *du.ve*                          'two'

     (e)  $^+$*sak.nāti* > $^+$*sak.knā.ti* > *sak.ku.ṇā.ti*
         '(he) can' (Skt. *śaknoti*)

Sometimes the cure is less radical but depends on the Consonantal Strength balance of the speech sounds in the head. Thus, in late Old High German initial /h/ but no stronger speech sound was dropped from head clusters.

(10) | Early OHG | Late OHG | NHG | |
     | --- | --- | --- | --- |
     | *hnīgan* | *nīgan* | *neigen* | 'to bow' |
     | *hlūt* | *lūt* | *laut* | 'loud' |
     | *hruofan* | *ruofan* | *rufen* | 'to call' |
     | *hwīz* | *wīz* | *weiß* | 'white' |

15

| | | | |
|---|---|---|---|
| *hunt* | *hunt* | *Hund* | 'dog' |
| *himil* | *himil* | *Himmel* | 'heaven' |
| *hagal* | *hagal* | *Hagel* | 'hail' |

In Italian, final vowels (glides) were lost in monotonic syllable heads of three, though not of two.

(11)  (a) *breve* > *brieve* > *breve* 'brief'
       *preca* > *prieca* > *preca* '(he) asks for'

      (b) *proba* > *pruova* > *prova* 'proof'
       *tropa* > *truova* > *trova* '(he) finds'

      (c) *Feb.rüar.io* > $^+$*Feb.brüa.io* > *Feb.bra.io* 'February'

      (d) (*Rienza, Rienzo, Rieti*)
       *rota* > *ruota* 'wheel'

An elegant way of shortening syllable heads is the amalgamation of speech sounds, a kind of consonantal monophthongization, as in Latin.

(12)  *düellum* > *bellum* 'war' (*duo* 'two')

Part (b) of the Head Law is manifest in the well-known strengthening changes of weak onsets, e.g. the strengthening of the vowels /i̯ u̯/ into the fricatives /j v/ in German:

(13)  /i̯ār/ > /jɑr/ *Jahr* 'year'
      /u̯al/ > /val/ *Wall* 'bulwark'

In Italian, /i̯/ is strengthened even further into the affricate /dʒ/, whereas /u̯/ has two strengthened reflexes: /v/, appearing mostly in words of Latin origin, and /gu̯/, appearing mostly in words of Germanic origin.

16

(14)  *ianuarius* > *gennaio* /dʒ–/ 'January'
     *destruere* > ⁺*dis.tru.i̯e.re* > *distrùggere* /–ddʒ–/
        'destroy'
     *u̯iu̯ere* > *vivere* 'to live'
     *u̯ad(an)* > *guad(are)* 'to wade through'
     *triu̯u̯a* > *trégua* 'truce'

In Dutch, onset /ɣ/ is strengthened by devoicing, yielding
/χ/.

(15)  [ɣēvən] > [χēvən] *geven* 'to give'

In Latin, ⁺/d/ became /t/ before ⁺/r/. As a consequence,
Latin does not have word-initial /dr/ except in borrowed
words, e.g. *draco̅* 'dragon' (from Gk. *dra̅ko̅n*).

(16)  *taedet* '(it) disgusts', *taeter/taetra* 'disgusting'
     Gk. *hydri̇́ā* 'water jug', Lat. *uter/utris* 'hose'
     Gk. *dri̅mýs* 'sharp, grim', OCS *dre̜su̯kŭ* 'sad',
     Lat. *tri̅stis* 'sad'

Though illustrating syllable-initial strengthening (assuming that the ⁺/dr/ cluster was everywhere tautosyllabic at
the time of the change), this example is best understood by
comparing it with part (c) of the Head Law: the strength
drop from [t] to [r] is sharper than from [d] to [r].

   Part (c) of the Head Law can be illustrated with word-
initial heads in Latin. They are here summarized following Zirin 1970: 27, 23.

(17)
$$
s \pm
\begin{Bmatrix}
\left.\begin{matrix} d \\ t \end{matrix}\right\} \pm r \\
k \\
\left.\begin{matrix} p \\ b \\ g \\ f \end{matrix}\right\} \pm r/l
\end{Bmatrix}
\qquad
s \pm
\left.\begin{matrix} g \\ k \\ s \end{matrix}\right\} \pm u̯
$$

It is easy to see that all monotonic clusters, i.e. all except those containing /s/ before plosives, consist of one of the strongest speech sounds followed by one of the weakest. Thus, only the clusters with the sharpest drop toward the Consonantal Strength of the nucleus, which must be a vowel in Latin, are allowed.

Good syllable heads according to the Head Law are those with a continual drop of Consonantal Strength from the beginning toward, and including, the nucleus. The reverse is true, as will be shown later, for codas. The preferred nuclei, as we shall see, are monophthongal. In summary, core syllables are distinguished as the preferred type of syllable by the preference laws. All language systems possess core syllables, and many possess no others, with languages tolerating only (C)V syllables (an optional head consonant followed by a monophthong) as the extreme case. Some languages permit a limited number of deviations from core structure. The most frequent "violators" are fricatives, chief among them [s]; in Latin /s/ is the only violator. Such violators may, sometimes together with their neighboring speech sounds, form quasi-syllables. In Latin, /s/ occurs by itself in word-initial quasi-syllables, where it is then quasi-nuclear; and there are no other quasi-syllables; e.g. /s|tā.re/ [$^\$$s̰,tā̄$^\$$rḛ$^\$$] *stare* 'to stand'. The special character of clusters with /s/ plus plosive in Latin becomes evident word-medially, viz. in simplicia, where they are divided, e.g. /mo$^\$$les$^\$$tus/ *molestus* 'troublesome'. This is shown by the fact that /s/ here makes position whereas a word-initial /s/ does not.[29] The quasi-syllabic character of Latin /s/ explains its development into an ordinary syllable in some of the Romance languages.

(18)  /$^\$$s̰,tā̄$^\$$re$^\$$/ > /$^\$$s$^\$$tā̄$^\$$re$^\$$/ > /$^\$$is$^\$$tā̄$^\$$re$^\$$/ >

   /$^\$$es$^\$$tar$^\$$/ *estar* 'to be' in Spanish

The core of the syllable with the basis /sta/ is freed of its prependix /s/ in the process; the syllable is changed into a core syllable. In Spanish all syllables are core syllables.

As the formulae in (17) show, the Latin clusters consisting of plosives plus liquids are those in (19).

(19) (a) pr  tr  kr          (b) pl  –  kl
         br  dr  gr               bl  –  gl

Many language systems have the gap */tl dl/, e.g. standard varieties of English generally and German at least word-initially. Faroese has (19) word-initially. Medially, only the clusters with a voiceless plosive can occur; intervocalically, they show the delightful distribution given in (20), cf. Vennemann 1978: 182–185.

(20) (a) $\bar{V}^\$prV$   $\bar{V}^\$trV$   $\bar{V}^\$krV$
      (b) $\bar{V}^\$plV$   $\breve{V}t^\$lV$   $\bar{V}^\$klV$

Latin used to have more syllable heads than those in (17). However, they were lost before the classical period, e.g. /gn/ in *gnātum* > *nātum* 'born', as happened to the analogous clusters in English.

(21)    E. *knee, gnome, gnat*; cf. G. *Knie* /kni/, *Gnom* /gnom/, (dial.) *Gnatze* /gnatsə/

Italian at one time in its history had syllable heads *(s)CR*, where *R* could be /i̯ u̯ r l/. The strongest of these, /l/, was weakened, mostly to /i̯/, sometimes (especially in dialects) to /r/.

(22)

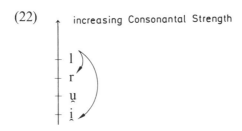

increasing Consonantal Strength

(23)   *plēnu* > *pieno* 'full'
       *blank* > *bianco* 'white' (from Germanic)
       *clave* > *chiave* /ki̯ave/ 'key'
       *glaciu* > *ghiaccio* /gi̯attʃo/ 'ice'
       *simila-* > *sim.la-* > *sem.bla-* >
                          ⎰*sem.bi̯a-, sembianza* 'semblance'
                          ⎱*sem.bra-, sembrare* 'to seem'
       *nebula* > *neb.la* > *neb.bla* >
                          ⎰*neb.bi̯a* 'fog'
                          ⎱*neb.bra* 'fog' (Abruzzese)

Clearly *CrV* and *Ci̯V* show stronger drops from *C* toward
*V* than *ClV*. Words such as *blu* 'blue' were borrowed after
these changes.

Classical Greek shows alternations of nasals and
homorganic voiced plosives, the latter occurring word-
initially before liquids. As a matter of fact, the clusters
/ml mr nl nr/ are prohibited word-initially in Greek.

(24)   *⁺mlit-i̯óh₂* > *blíttō* 'I take away the honey'; cf. Gk.
       *méli, mélitos* (stem *melit-*), Hittite *milit*, Lat. *mel,
       mellis* (< *⁺melt-*), OIr. *mil*, Goth. *miliþ* (all
       'honey'), and possibly E. *mildew*

       *⁺mro-tós* > *brotós* 'mortal man'; cf. *⁺á-mrotós*
       > *⁺ám.ro.tos* > *ám.bro.tos* 'immortal', Lat.
       *morī* 'to die', *mortuus* 'dead', Skt. *márate* '(he)
       dies', *mr̥táh̥* 'dead', *mártah̥* 'mortal', E. *murder*, etc.

$^+$*nr-ṓps* > *drṓps* (in Hesychios); cf. Gk. *anḗr*, $^+$*an.rós* > *an.drós*, *anéra* 'man (nom., gen., acc.)', Skt. *nr̥-*, acc. *náram* 'man', Gk. *ōp-s* 'eye, face, countenance'

$^+$*nl-* (no examples)

The drop from a plosive to a liquid is certainly sharper than that from a nasal.

When syllable heads of / h / plus another speech sound were simplified by / h /-deletion in English – as they were in Old High German, cf. (10) – the best of them, / hu̯ /, as in *what* / hu̯at /, was preserved longer and still survives in many varieties of English.

# The Coda Law

(25) **Coda Law**
A syllable coda is the more preferred: (a) the smaller the number of speech sounds in the coda, (b) the less the Consonantal Strength of its offset, and (c) the more sharply the Consonantal Strength drops from the offset toward the Consonantal Strength of the preceding syllable nucleus.

Part (a) of the Coda Law shows its most dramatic effects in word-final syllables. Word-final clusters in Sanskrit are, with one exception to which I shall return, reduced to their onsets, which are the weakest elements in the groups.

(26)

| Nominative | Accusative | |
|---|---|---|
| *adan* | *adantam* | 'eating' |
| *pumān* | *pumāṃsam* | 'man' |
| *anvaṅ* | *anvañcam* | 'following' |

Actually the cluster reduced in *adan* for example was $^+nts$, cf. Lat. *edēns/edentem* 'eating'. An extreme example is $^+a$ $+chānd+s+t >$ *achān* '(it) seemed (3rd sg. ind. augmented sigmatic aorist)'. Afrikaans similarly deletes final alveolar plosives after fricatives and plosives.

(27)

| Singular | Plural | |
|---|---|---|
| *hoof* | *hoofde* | 'chief(s)' |
| *voog* /-x/ | *voogde* | 'guardian(s)' |
| *kuns* | *kunste* | 'art(s)' |
| *resep* | *resepte* | 'recipe(s)' |
| *konflik* | *konflikte* | 'conflict(s)' |

Dutch and German preserve the final plosive: *hoofd*, *Haupt*; *kunst*, *Kunst*; etc. In the prehistory of Greek, all final consonants except $^+/$s n r$/$ were lost.

(28)

| Nominative | Genitive | |
|---|---|---|
| *méli* | *mélitos* | 'honey' |
| *klíma* | *klímatos* | 'slope' |
| *gérōn* | *gérontos* | 'old man' |

The vocative of *ánax/ánaktos* 'lord' is simplified accordingly: $^+$*ánakt* > *ána*. In English, there are tendencies to delete the only remaining voiced plosive, /d/, after its homorganic nasal, yielding such popular rimes as *fine/ mind, down/ground*. (/b/ and /g/ had long been lost in *lamb*, *sing* etc.) Moreover, final /t/ tends to be lost after all obstruents, as in *kep'*, *slep'*, *fis'*, *dentis'*.

In Icelandic, consonants are easily lost from both medial and final codas, especially with a little help from assimilation. The second and third columns show inflectional, derivational, and compositional forms of those in the first, which are glossed.

(29) | | | | |
|---|---|---|---|---|
| *hestur* | *hestbak* | *hests* | 'horse' |
| /hɛs.tʏr/ | /hɛs.bak/ | /hɛss/ | |
| *falskur* | | *fals(k)t* | 'false' |
| /fals.kʏr/ | | /falst/ | |
| *kemba* | *kem(b)da* | *kem(b)t* | 'to comb' |
| /kem.ba/ | /kem.da/ | /kemt/ | |
| *sandur* | | *san(d)s* | 'sand' |
| /san.dʏr/ | | /sans/ | |
| *margur* | | *margt* | 'many' |
| /mar.gʏr/ | | /mart/ | |
| *hálfur* | *hál(f)ra* | *hál(f)s* | 'half' |
| /haul.vʏr/ | /haul.ra/ | /hauls/ | |
| *bragð* | | *brag(ð)s* | 'trick' |
| /braɣð/ | | /braxs/ | |
| *jafn* | | *jafnt* | 'even' |
| /jabn/ | | /jaft, jamt/ | |
| *hrafn* | | *hrafns* | 'raven' |
| /hrabn/ | | /hrafs/ | |
| *vatn* | | *vatns* | 'water' |
| /vatn/ | | /vass/ | |
| *barn* | | *barns* | 'child' |
| /badn/ | | /bass/ | |
| *verr* | *versna* | | 'worse' |
| /vɛrr/ | /vɛs.na/ | | |

Italian too shows loss of consonants from complex codas.

(30)  *sextu* > *ses.to*  'sixth'
      *iunxi* > *giun.si*  'I have reached'
      *punctu* > *pun.to*  'point'

In monosyllables, final /s/ weakened into /i̯/ in Italian:

(31)   *post* > $^+$*pos* > *poi*   'afterwards'
      *nos* > *noi*         'us'
      *vos* > *voi*         'you-all'

Finally, it may be mentioned that Italian has eliminated (excepting some loan words and truncated forms) all word-final consonants, some by vocalization as in (31) but most by loss, a few by adding a protective vowel.

(32)   *patrem* > *padre*   'father'
      *cantat* > *canta*  '(he) sings'
      *fac*    > *fa*     'make!'
      *dic*    > *di'*    'say!'
      *sunt*   > *sono*  'they are'

Part (b) of the Coda Law is evident in the relative Strength of the correlates of speech sounds in initial head and final coda position. Best known is the difference between the strong aspirate correlates of English voiceless plosives as onsets of words and stressed syllables and their weak, unaspirated, and unreleased correlates in syllable-final position.

(33)   *pet* [p$^h$ɛt$^1$], *cap* [k$^h$æp$^1$], *tick* [t$^h$ɪk$^1$], compare
      *patrol* [p$^h$ə.t$^h$róu̯l] etc.

Such weakness is typically the bridge toward loss of oral articulation, yielding a glottal stop, as in the Cockney dialect (Sivertsen 1960: 111–118).

(34)   *quite a lot* [kwayʔ ə lɔʔ]
      *a group* [ə grü:ʔ]
      *a new book* [ə nü: buʔ]
      *collect* [kleʔ]
      *kept* [keʔ]

Fricatives may likewise weaken and lose their oral articulation, as in Sanskrit and in Spanish dialects.

(35)
| Nominative | Accusative | |
|---|---|---|
| *apāḥ* | *apasam* | 'active' |
| *āśīḥ* | *āśiṣam* | 'prayer' |
| *cakṣuḥ* | *cakṣuṣam* | 'seeing' |

(36)
| Standard | Dialect | |
|---|---|---|
| *salas* | *salah* | 'halls' |
| *estilos* | *ehtiloh* | 'styles' |
| *esnupi* | *ehnupi* | 'Snoopy' |

In Chinese, all syllable-final plosives and fricatives were lost via [ʔ] and [h], respectively, with tonogenesis as part of the process.

In the Romance languages we find /p/ and /b/ weakening into /u̯/, /t/ and /d/ into /i̯/, and /k/ and /g/ into /u̯/ or /i̯/ under various conditions.

(37)  Span. *cap.ti.vu* > *cau̯.ti.vo* 'captive'
Span. *pec.tu* > *pei̯.to* > *pecho* /pe.čo/ 'breast'
Ital. *bi.be.re* > *beb.re* > *beu̯.re* > be.re 'to drink'
Fr. *fra.tre* > *frad.re* > *frai̯.re* > *frère* 'brother'
Fr. *cre.de.re* > *cred.re* > *crei̯.re* > *croire* 'to believe'
Ital. *in.teg.ru* > *in.tei̯.ro* > *in.te.ro* 'entire'

In many languages /l/ weakens to /r/, /u̯/, or /i̯/.

(38)  Ital. *hu.mi.li.ta.te* > *u.mil.tà* 'humility'/ *o.mer.tà* 'discretion'
Ital. *col.lo.ca* > *col.ca* > *cor.ca* > *co.ri.ca* 'lies down'

And. *hu̯el.ga* > *hu̯er.ga* 'rest, repose'
  *al.ma* > *ar.ma* 'soul'
Span. *local(e)* > *lugar* 'place'
Gk. *a.ðel.fós* > *a.ðer.fós* 'brother'
Fr. *al.ba* > *au̯.bə* > /ob/ 'dawn'
Bav. *ba̤l* > *ba̤o̤i̯* 'ball'
  *fil* > *fu̯i̯* 'much'

These types of change – as well as the weakening of nasals to nasal vowels, or nasality on vowels – not only apply to offsets but also to non-final coda consonants; e.g. Bavarian /kald̦/ > /kɔid̦/ 'cold'. The same is also true for the vocalization of /r/ in many English and Northern German dialects, and for /l/, e.g. *milk* [mɪṷk], in certain varieties of English.

The most impressive example of coda weakening is Klingenheben's Law for Haussa (Klingenheben 1928).

(39) Labials⎫
   Velars ⎬ > *u̯*⎫
   Dentals  > *r*⎭ in codas

(40) ⁺*ma.kaf.ni.ya* > *ma.kaw.ni.ya* 'a blind one (fem.)'; *ma.kā.fo* (masc.)
  ⁺*ta.lak.či* > *ta.law.či* 'poverty'; *ta.la.ka* 'a poor one'
  ⁺*hag.ni* > *haw.ni* 'left side'; *ba.ha.go* 'a left-handed one'
  ⁺*fat.ke* > *far.ke* 'merchant'; *fa.tā.ke* (pl.)
  ⁺*ma.z(a).ma.za* > *mar.ma.za* 'very fast'; *ma.za* 'fast'
  ⁺*hal.se* > *har.še* 'tongue'; *ha.lu.sa* (pl.)
  ⁺*hat* > *har* 'until' (borrowed from Arabic)

I mentioned earlier the rule that Sanskrit word-final codas

may contain only single consonants. This rule has one exception: /r/ followed by a plosive (only voiceless plosives are allowed word-finally at the end of an expression uttered in isolation).

(41)  *āvart* '(he) turned' (root *vr̥t*)
      *amārṭ* '(he) was wiping' (root *mr̥j*)
      *vark* '(he) bent' (root *vr̥j*)
      *ūrk* 'strength (nom. sg.)'

These groups show the weakest consonant of the language system followed by one of the strongest. The drop from a voiceless plosive to /r/ in the direction of a vowel is thus the sharpest possible in the language. Part (c) of the Coda Law allows us to understand this singular exception to an otherwise general rule.

# The Nucleus Law

(42)  **Nucleus Law**
      A nucleus is the more preferred: (a) the steadier its speech sound, and (b) the less the Consonantal Strength of its speech sound.

Part (a) expresses the idea that monophthongs are preferred to diphthongs, which in turn are preferred to triphthongs. That this is true is evident from the fact that the relatively few languages with triphthongs such as Portuguese also have diphthongs, and languages with diphthongs also have monophthongs, while the converse implications do not hold. Steadying of polyphthongs is predicted by the law. Indeed, monophthongizations occur in abundance in both the Germanic and the Romance languages as well as in many others. A few examples may suffice.

(43)  (a)  $^{+}e\underset{.}{i} > \bar{\imath}$ from Proto-Indo-European to Germanic
OHG, OS, OE *stīgan*, OIcel., OFris. *stīga*, Goth. *steigan* (where *ei* represents /ī/) 'to go upwards, rise, climb'; cf. Gk. *steîkʰō* 'I stride'

(b)  $^{+}ai > \bar{a}$ in Old English
OE *stān* 'stone'; cf. OHG *stain, stein*, OIcel. *steinn*

(c)  $^{+}ai$, $^{+}au > \bar{a}$ in Frisian
OFris, *twā* 'two', *āge* 'eye'; cf. OHG *zwei*, OIcel. *tvei-*, OE *twā*, OHG *augo, ougo*, OIcel. *auga*, OE *ēage*

(d)  $^{+}ai$, $^{+}au > \bar{e}$, $\bar{o}$ in Old Saxon (except before $\underset{.}{i}$, $\underset{.}{u}$)
OS *stēn* 'stone', *ōg* 'eye'; cf. (b), (c)

(e)  *ie̜, uo̜, ye̜* $> \bar{\imath}$, $\bar{u}$, $\bar{y}$ in Middle German (and the standard language)
MHG *liebe, muot, güete*, Standard German *Liebe* (where *ie* now represents /ī/), *Mut*, *Güte* 'love, mood, goodness'

(44)  (a)  $^{+}ei > \bar{\imath}$; $^{+}oi > \bar{u}$ ($\bar{\imath}$ after $\underset{.}{u}$ and in final syllables);
$^{+}eu$, $^{+}ou > \bar{u}$ between Proto-Indo-European and Classical Latin
*deicō* $> d\bar{\imath}co$ 'I say' (Gk. *deík-nȳ-mi* 'I show')
*oinus* $> \bar{u}nus$ 'one' (Gk. *oinế* 'ace')
$^{+}\underset{.}{u}oikois > v\bar{\imath}c\bar{\imath}s$ 'villages (dat.)' (Gk. *oîkois*)
$^{+}deukō > doucō > d\bar{u}cō$ 'I lead' (Goth. *tiuhan*)

$^+$*louk-s* > *lūx* 'light', $^+$*louk-nā* > *lūna* 'moon' (Gk. *leukós* 'white')

$^+$*pro-v(i)dēns* > $^+$*proudēns* > *prūdēns* 'prudent'

(b) $^+$*ai* > *ei* > *ī*, $^+$*au* > *ū* in Latin non-initial syllables

   $^+$*cecaidī* > *cecīdī* 'I have cut' (*caedō* 'I cut')

   $^+$*incaidō* > *inceidō* > *incīdō* 'I cut into'

   $^+$*-ais* > *-eis* > *-īs* (dat. pl. of *ā*-stems, Gk. *-ais*)

(c) *ae* > *ɛ̄*, *au* > *ɔ̄* in rural Latin

   *praetor* > *pretor* 'chief magistrate'

   *haedus* > *hedus* 'young goat, kid'

   *aurum* > *orum* 'gold'

   *lautus* > *lotus* 'elegant'

(d) *ae* > *ɛ*, *au* > *ɔ* in most Romance languages, a continuation of (c), e.g. in Italian

   *spaera* > *sfera, spera* 'globe, ball'

   *maestu* > *mesto* 'sad'

   *quaero* > *chero, chiedo* '(I) demand'

   *causa* > *cosa* 'thing'

   *pauperu* > *povero* 'poor'

   *thesauru* > *tesoro* 'treasure'

(e) Monophthongization in newly arising diphthongs, e.g. Ital. *fa.bu.la* > *fab.la* > *fau̯.la* > *fo.la* 'fairy tale'

Part (b) of the Nucleus Law is evident in the fact that most languages tolerate only vowels as nuclei, e.g. Latin, Italian, and Proto-Germanic; some, vowels plus [r], e.g. some Slavic languages; some these plus [l], e.g. Sanskrit. Standard varieties of German and English permit only vowels as nuclei of stressed syllables, but vowels, liquids, and nasals as nuclei of unstressed syllables. Some languages on the North West Coast of the North American continent even permit obstruents, including voiceless plosives, as nuclei. (Cf. Hoard 1978; Bell 1978, where certain mismatches between nucleability and Consonantal Strength are also pointed out.)

# The Weight Law

(45) **Weight Law**

In stress accent languages an accented syllable is the more preferred, the closer its syllable weight is to two moras, and an unaccented syllable is the more preferred the closer its weight is to one mora. (The optimal stressed syllable is bimoric, the optimal unstressed syllable is unimoric.)

This law, which may also be called the Stressed Syllable Law or Prokosch's Law, may be illustrated with Prokosch's own examples (1939: 140).

(46)  (a)  *ne.men* '(we) take' $\left.\right\}$ > $\bar{V}$
$\phantom{(46)  (a)  }$ *nā.men* '(we) took'

$\phantom{(46)  }$ (b)  *dah.te* '(he) covered' $\left.\right\}$ > $\breve{V}$
$\phantom{(46)  (b)  }$ *dāh.te* '(he) thought'

"This means that MHG accented syllables had either one or two or three time units – short vowel without consonant, short vowel with consonant, long vowel without consonant, long vowel with consonant. In Standard NHG, leaving aside complicated details, it may be said that every accented syllable has two time units – short vowel with consonant, or long vowel without consonant." By contrast, the tendency to shorten unstressed syllables to one mora is evident in the history of all the Germanic languages.

Italian shows the same kind of development. I cite Genot's summary of the facts (1979: 19): "En latin vulgaire, les syllabes (c'est-à-dire essentiellement les voyelles) toniques ont tendu à s'allonger, et les syllabes (i.e. voyelles) atones ont tendu à s'abréger:

(47)

| LATIN | phase intermédiaire | ITALIEN |
|---|---|---|
| | longue ⟶ longue | |
| syll. tonique | | syll. tonique |
| | brève  s'allonge  longue | |
| | brève ⟶ brève | |
| syll. atone | | syll. atone |
| | longue  s'abrège  brève | |

... On a en fin de compte, en italien, une corrélation entre tonique et longue, atone et brève." That the redistribution of length is not so much a matter of vowels but of syllables is evident in the fact that / ɛ ɔ / are diphthongized in Italian grosso modo only in stressed open syllables but not in stressed closed syllables (never in unstressed syllables). All examples bear stress on the first syllable.

(48)  ɛ > ɛɛ > eɛ > e̥ɛɛ > i̥ɛɛ = i̥ɛ̄
      ɔ > ɔɔ > oɔ > o̥ɔɔ > u̥ɔɔ = u̥ɔ̄
      in stressed open syllables

(49)  pĕ.de  >  piede / pi̯ɛ̄.de /   'foot'
      lĕ.ve  >  lieve / ʎɛ̄.ve /   'light'

      fŏ.cu  >  fuoco / fu̯ɔ̄.ko /   'fire'
      rŏ.ta  >  ruota / ru̯ɔ̄.ta /   'wheel'

(50)  *dĕn.te* > *dente* /dɛn.te/  'tooth'
      *pĕc.tu* > *petto* /pɛt.to/  'breast'
      *pŏr.ta* > *porta* /pɔr.ta/  'door'
      *nŏc.te* > *notte* /nɔt.te/  'night'

Open syllable lengthening of nuclei is, of course, a widespread phenomenon. It occurs only in stress accent languages, and there only in stressed syllables. The Weight Law thus explains why the combination of contrastive nuclear length and a stress accent are universally disfavored, whereas in pitch accent languages and tone languages contrastive nuclear length is commonplace.

# The Law of Initials

(51)  **Law of Initials**
      Word-medial syllable heads are the more preferred, the less they differ from possible word-initial syllable heads of the language system.

In Classical Latin, every medial syllable head is a possible word-initial syllable head. The converse is not true; for example, clusters of /s/ and a plosive are possible at the beginning of words and there do not make position, whereas medially they are always heterosyllabic and thus do make position.[30] Italian, too, is in perfect agreement with the Law of Initials, as far as I can see.

German abides by the Law of Initials rather well, but allows for a small number of exceptions which have arisen from recent syncopations. Thus, word-initial clusters of alveolar plosives and the lateral liquid are not allowed; in non-initial syllables they occur in the refined standard language and in Southern pronunciation, but in my own

Northern pronunciation they are heterosyllabicated, as is evident in the syllable-final devoicing of /d/ before /l/.

(52)  *han.de.lung > han.dlung > han/t/.lung* 'action'
      *e.de.le > e.dle > e/t/.le* 'noble ones'

English disallows word-initial /tl dl θl/ while permitting /tr dr θr/; medial syllabications follow suit.

(53)  *a.trocious*          *At.lantic*
      *a.droit, a.drenal*   *ad.lib, Ad.lerian*
      *ar.thritis*          *ath.letic*

## The Law of Finals

(54)  **Law of Finals**
      Word-medial syllable codas are the more pre-
      ferred, the less they differ from possible word-final
      syllable codas of the language system.

This is a very weak law that allows for numerous exceptions. For instance, Standard Italian does not allow any
consonants at the end of ordinary words, but medially all
consonants may occur as syllable offsets, though they
have to obey severe contact restrictions.

Nevertheless, peculiar changes may occur that would
be hard to understand except in relation to the Law of
Finals. For example, Sanskrit, as well as several related
Indic languages, doubles consonants after /r/ in medial
clusters. Viewed in isolation, this change makes no sense
whatsoever; it simply is not an ordinary type of sound
change. It is all the more peculiar in view of the fact that
the general rule in these languages is for consonants to
double *before* other consonants.

(55)  *ad.ya > ad.dya*          'today'
      *pret.ya > pret.tya*      'post-mortal state'
      *put.reṇa > put.treṇa*    'son (instr.)'
      *sap.ta- > sap.pta-*      'seven'
      *ak.tubhiḥ > ak.ktubhiḥ*  'at night'

(56)  *mār.gam > mārg.gam*      'concerning game'
      *var.gam > varg.gam*      'defender, section,
                                 group'
      *dīr.gha- > dīrg.gha-*    'wide, long'
      *ar.kaḥ > ark.kaḥ*        'sun'
      *ār.ta > ārt.ta*          'concerned'

The contemporary Indian grammarian Siddheshwar
Varma (1961: 62–64) gives an excellent explanation for
this apparent conflict: "There is no doubt that in the
above examples the first member of the group – viz., *r* –
has not been doubled, and it may prima facie appear as if
it was an exception to the rule of syllabification given
above [the rule that, e.g., *putram* is *puttram* qua *put$tram*,
T.V.]; but a closer reflection will show that even here the
same tendency has worked – viz., that of keeping the first
syllable close [i.e. closed, T.V.], so that *svarggam* was divided as *svarg/gam*. The first syllable here could not be
closed with *r*, because there exists no word in Sanskrit that
ends in *r* at the end of a sentence." Doubling of the following consonant is thus a device for bringing syllables ending in /r/ in line with the Law of Finals; because whereas
/r/ is not allowed in Sanskrit as a word-final offset, the
group /r/ plus plosive is allowed in word-final position, as
I showed earlier when illustrating part (c) of the Coda
Law in (41).

     The only other consonant that behaves like /r/ in the
Sanskrit gemination is /s/, and as may be expected, /s/
shares with /r/ the property of being banned from word-

final position (in pause and most other contexts); cf. Varma 1961: 75.

(57)  *has.ta-* > *hast.ta-*                    'hand'
      *puṣ.ṭa-* > *puṣṭ.ṭa-*                    'wealth'
      *a.vas.kan.da-* > *a.vask.kan.da-*  'assault'

## The Strength Assimilation Law

(58)  **Strength Assimilation Law**
      If Consonantal Strength is assimilated in a syllable
      contact, the Consonantal Strength of the stronger
      speech sound decreases.

The Strength Assimilation Law is an attempted generalization of Murray's Progressive Assimilation Law (1982:
171, 182f.).

(59)  **Progressive Assimilation Law**
      In progressive assimilation, the speech sound
      with lesser Consonantal Strength dominates.

Murray illustrates his law chiefly with examples from
Italian dialects which he takes from Rohlfs 1972: 400.

(60)  *r.l* > *r.r*
      Ital. *Carlo*, Sic. *Carru* 'Charles'

      *r.n* > *r.r*
      Ital. *forno*, Cors. *fòrru* 'oven'

      *l.n* > *l.l*
      OFr. *jalne*, Ital. *giallo* 'yellow'

      *l.d* > *l.l*
      Ital. *calda*, Latium *calla* 'warm (fem.)'

$m.b > m.m$
Ital. *sambuco*, Sic. *sammuco* 'elder'

$n.d > n.n$
Ital. *mondo*, Sic. *munnu* 'world'

$ŋ.g > ŋ.ŋ$
Ital. *lungo*, Sic. *lònnu* 'long'

The pre-history of Latin provides additional examples.

(61)　$^+l.d > l.l$
　　$^+saldō > sallō$ 'I salt' (E. *salt*)
　　$^+l.n > l.l$
　　$^+kolnis > collis$ 'hill' (Lith. *kalnas*)
　　$^+l.s > {}^+l.z > l.l$
　　$^+vel\text{-}se > velle$ 'to want' (compare *es-se*)
　　$^+r.s > {}^+r.z > r.r$
　　$^+fer\text{-}se > ferre$ 'to carry'

In the systematic exceptions $^+ager\text{-}los > agellus$ 'little field', $^+puer\text{-}la > puella$ 'girl' etc., the shape of the diminutive suffix was preserved by analogy.

The pre-history of Germanic also furnishes similar examples.

(62) (a) $^+l.n > l.l, ll, l$
　　　Goth. *fulls*, OE, OS *full*, OHG *fol, follēr*; cf.
　　　　Skt. *pūrṇaḥ*, Lith. *pìlnas*, Lat. *plēnus* 'full'
　　　Goth. *wulla,* OIcel. *ull*, OE *wull*, OHG *wolla*;
　　　　cf. Skt. *ūrṇā*, Lith. *vìlna*, OCS *vlŭna* 'wool'

　　(b) $^+r.n > r.r, r$
　　　Goth. *fairra*, OIcel. *fiarre*, OE *feor*, OHG
　　　　*ferro*, OS *fer* 'far'; cf. Goth. *fairneis* 'old',
　　　　OS *fern* 'past', OHG *firni* 'old, dated'

OE *steorra*, OHG *sterro*; cf. Goth. *stairnō*,
OIcel. *stiarna*, OHG *sterno* 'star'

Sidamo, a Cushitic language, assimilates a suffixal onset
/n/ if the preceding consonant is weaker (it uses a different device if it is stronger, see (98) below):

(63)   *mar-nónni* → *mar.rónni*   'they went'
       *ful-némmo* → *ful.lémmo*   'we go out'

One might want to cite the changes $^{+}$/bn/ > /pp/, $^{+}$/dn/
> /tt/, $^{+}$/gn/ > /kk/, $^{+}$/nu̯/ > /nn/ in the pre-history of
Germanic as well as similar apparent cases of progressive
assimilation in Pāli as counterexamples. However, Murray (1982) has shown that the Pāli changes actually reflect
gemination plus syllable head simplification; cf. the
examples in (9.c,e). It follows that they tell us nothing
about progressive assimilation. I will tentatively propose
the same kind of interpretation for the Germanic
materials in my exemplification of the Contact Law; cf.
(85).

It seems, therefore, that Murray's Law and thus the
"progressive" part of the Strength Assimilation Law is
well supported. But there exist very instructive examples
for its "regressive" part as well. Latin is especially
generous.

(64)   (a)  $^{+}t.s$ > $s.s$
            $^{+}$*met-suī* > *messui* 'I have mowed' (*metō*)

       (b)  $^{+}p.m$ > $^{+}b.m$ > $m.m$
            $^{+}$*sup-mos* > *summus* 'highest' (Gk. *hupó-*)

       (c)  $^{+}p.n$ > $^{+}b.n$ > $m.n$
            $^{+}$*su̯ep-nos* > *somnus* 'sleep' (Skt. *svapnaḥ*)

       (d)  $^{+}k.m$ > $^{+}g.m$ > $ŋ.m$
            $^{+}$*sek.mentom* > *segmentum* [ŋ.m] 'section'
            (*secō*)

(e) $^+k.n$ > $^+g.n$ > $ŋ.n$
$^+dek$-$nos$ > $dignus$ [$ŋ.n$] 'dignified' (*decet*)

(f) $^+t.n$ > $^+d.n$ > $n.n$
$^+atnos$ > $annus$ 'year' (Goth. *aþn*)

(g) $^+d.m$ > $m.m$
$^+rād$-$mos$ > $^+rāmmos$ > $rāmus$ 'branch'
(*rādix*)

(h) $^+d.l$ > $l.l$
$^+sed$-$lā$ > $sella$ 'seat' (*sedeō*)

(i) $^+n.l$ > $l.l$
$^+korōn$-$lā$ > $corōlla$ 'little crown, garland'
(*corōna*)
$^+kon$-$legō$ > $colligō$ 'I gather'

(j) $^+b.r$ > $r.r$
$^+sub$-$ripiō$ > $surripiō$ 'I take away'

(k) $^+d.r$ > $r.r$
$^+ad$-$ripiō$ > $arripiō$ 'I seize'

(l) $^+n.r$ > $r.r$
$^+kon$-$rumpō$ > $corrumpō$ 'I destroy'

The pre-history of Germanic offers similar examples.

(65) (a) $^+d.l$ > $l.l, ll, l$

$^+mad.la$- > $^+mal.la$-; Germ.-Lat. *mallus*
'law court', *mallare* 'to accuse, prosecute';
cf. $^+maþ$-$la$- (> $^+mag.la$-) in Goth. *maþl*
'convention place', *maþljan* 'to talk', OIcel.
*mál* (< $^+mahl$) 'speech, law-suit', OE *mæðl*
'council, assembly', *mæðlian* 'to speak, ha-
rangue', OHG *mahal*, in compounds *madal*-

$^+stad.la$- > $^+stal.la$-; OIcel. *stallr*, OE
*steall*, OHG *stal, stalles* 'stall, stable'; cf.

$^+stap.la$- in OE *staðol*, OHG *stadel* 'barn, shed', Skt. *sthatram* ($^+l > r$) 'place, position'

$^+k\bar{\imath}d\text{-}la\text{-} > {}^+k\bar{\imath}l.la\text{-} > {}^+k\bar{\imath}.la$- in OHG *k\bar{\imath}l*, NHG *Keil* 'wedge'; cf. $^+k\bar{\imath}p.la$- in NHG (dial.) *keidel* (id.)

(b) $^+z.l > l.l, ll, l$

$^+knuz.lian > {}^+knul.lian$; OIcel. *knylla* 'to beat', OE *knyllan* 'to push'; cf. $^+knus(i)an$ in OIcel. *knosa* 'to beat', OE *cnyssan*, OHG *khnussen* 'to push'

$^+hruz.lan > {}^+hrul.lan$; OIcel. *hrolla* 'to tremble, shiver'; cf. $^+hreusan$ in OIcel. *hriósa* 'to shudder', Gk. *krýos* 'frost' ($< {}^+krýsos$, cf. *krýs-tallos* 'ice')

(c) $^+z.m > {}^+m.m, mm, m$

$^+paz.ma\text{-} > {}^+pam.ma\text{-}, {}^+ez.ma\text{-} > {}^+em.ma\text{-}$; Goth. *pamma, imma* (dat. sg. masc. of dem. and 3rd pers. pron.); cf. Skt. dat. *tasmai, asmai*, abl. *tasmāt, asmāt*

$^+ez.mi > {}^+em.mi$; Goth. *im* '(I) am'; cf. Gk. *eimí* (Lesb. *émmi*), OCS *jesmĭ*, Skt. *asmi* '(I) am'

I believe that in regressive Strength assimilation we will find many exceptions. But in evaluating such cases we should keep two caveats in mind. First, where the syllable boundary coincides with a morphological boundary, the direction of assimilation may be determined by a desire to protect the integrity of a stem or affix. Second, as already noted, syllable offsets are typically weaker than syllable onsets. As a matter of fact, they may weaken to the point where they are little more than an indistinct mora bearer. To fill this mora with a copy of the following onset appears to be a natural strategy which may have to be kept distinct from genuine Strength assimilation; cf. the instructive Andalusian examples provided by Lapesa (1965: 324).

(66)  *bur.la* > *buh.la* > *bul.la* 'mockery'
      *car.ne* > *cah.ne* > *can.ne* 'flesh'

In any event, it seems to me that as a preference law the generalized Strength Assimilation Law stands a good chance of being valid. And that would not even be very surprising: It would be a special application of the well-known fact that – setting apart special cases such as the margins of medial stressed syllables – word-medial consonants are generally weaker than word-initial consonants.

# The Contact Law

(67)  **Contact Law**
      A syllable contact $A^\$B$ is the more preferred, the less the Consonantal Strength of the offset A and the greater the Consonantal Strength of the onset B; more precisely – the greater the characteristic difference $CS(B) - CS(A)$ between the Consonantal Strength of B and that of A.

Let me begin my illustration of the Contact Law with a very simple example taken from German. Consider the syllabication of the words (names) *Wartha* (basis / varta /) and *Tatra* (basis / tatra /). Assume that a formal numerical theory of Consonantal Strength for German assigns the speech sounds / r / and / t / – or their positional phonetic correlates in both words – the values $\alpha$ and $\beta$, respectively:

$CS(r) = \alpha$, $CS(t) = \beta$. Remembering that $/r/$ is a very weak speech sound and $/t/$ a very strong one, we know that $\alpha$ will be a small number, let us assume 4 for the sake of concrete illustration, and $\beta$ a large one, let us assume 10. Let us now compare the characteristic difference of the two contacts $/r^\$t/$ and $/t^\$r/$. That of the former is $CS(t) - CS(r) = \beta - \alpha = 10 - 4 = 6$; that of the latter $CS(r) - CS(t) = \alpha - \beta = 4 - 10 = -6$. Therefore the contact $/r^\$t/$ is greatly preferred over the contact $/t^\$r/$ according to the Contact Law. The two German examples are in harmony with this evaluation, as shown by their syllabications.

(68)   *Wartha* $/\text{var}^\$\text{ta}/$, *Tatra* $/\text{ta}^\$\text{tra}/$

As a matter of fact, the contact $/t^\$r/$ does not exist in German simplex words; wherever it occurs, the syllable boundary coincides with a morpheme boundary. Note that whereas $/t^\$r/$ would make a bad contact because of the very small value of $CS(r) - CS(t)$, $/tr/$ makes a good syllable head by virtue of the very same fact, because a syllable head $^\$AB$ is the more preferred the smaller is the difference $CS(B) - CS(A)$, or the greater that of $CS(A) - CS(B)$, viz. according to part (c) of the Head Law. By contrast, $/rt/$ would make a very bad syllable head, and indeed German does not tolerate this head under any circumstances.

The example given illustrates at once a much more general syllabication rule for German (cf. Vennemann 1982: 302):

(69)   **Morpho-Syllabic Theorem for Contemporary Standard German**
       If the syllable boundary does not lie before or within the last Consonantal Strength class peak, even though this would be allowed by the other

phonological rules, the syllable boundary coincides with a morphological boundary.

(A Consonantal Strength class peak is a speech sound occurrence within a speech sound sequence that is not flanked by a speech sound from a higher Consonantal Strength class.)

Let us consider one additional pair of exemples. Clusters of a voiceless plosive P and the lateral liquid /l/ may be either tautosyllabic or heterosyllabic after tense vowels.

(70)  $/\bar{V}^\$PlV/, /\bar{V}P^\$lV/$

(71)  *eklig* /e.klıç/ 'disgusting', *täglich* /täk.lıç/ 'daily'

Tautosyllabication is the simplex syllabication, just as for the corresponding clusters with /r/, cf. *Tatra* in (68).

(72)  *Thekla* /té.klɑ/, *Kaplan* /kɑ.plán/, *Oklahoma* /o.klɑ.hó.mɑ/

Heterosyllabication by contrast presupposes the coincidence of a morpheme boundary.

(73)  *täg-lich* /täk.lıç/ 'daily'
      *klag-los* /klɑk.los/ 'without complaint'
      *kritik-los* /kri.tik.los/ 'uncritical'
      *lieb-lich* /lip.lıç/ 'lovely'
      *lieb-reich* /lip.raıç/ 'lovely'
      *Not-ruf* /not.ruf/ 'emergency call'

As a diachronic application of the Contact Law along the lines of the Diachronic Maxim (1), the interpretation of the West Germanic gemination in Murray and Vennemann 1983 may be cited. The essence of the change is contained in (74).

(74) **West Germanic Consonant Gemination in the Structure V̆CRV**

    (a) If R is a "semivowel", all C's except $^{+}$/r/ are geminated:
        Goth. *satjan, -skapjan*; OS *settian, skeppian*
        Goth. *kunjis, halja*; OS *kunnies, hellia*
        Goth. *farjan*, OS *ferian*
        Goth. *naqaþs*; OHG *nackot*
        ON *gørva*, OS *gerwean*, NHG *gerben*

    (b) If R is a liquid, only voiceless plosive C's are geminated:
        Goth. *akrs*, ON *eple*; OS *akkar*, OE *æppel*
        Goth. *ligrs, nadrs, fugls*; OHG *legar, natra*
        ($^{+}d > t$), *fogal*[31]

Proto-Germanic had inherited from Proto-Indo-European a very simple rule of syllabication:

(75) Internuclear clusters of two are heterosyllabic after short vowels.

This rule is optimal with regard to simplicity but not with regard to naturalness. Only heterosyllabic contacts with a weak first element and a strong second element are good; as the Consonantal Strength of the first element increases and that of the second decreases, so that the characteristic difference of the contact decreases, the contact becomes less and less preferred. The very worst contacts are those with a vowel (or "semivowel") as second element. They are always changed by geminating the first element. The result is an improved contact – equal Strength on both sides of the boundary – plus a new, very good syllable head:

(76)   $-\breve{V}C^\$\underset{\sim}{V}V- \; > \; -\breve{V}C^\$C\underset{\sim}{V}V-$

Only $^+/r/$ is exempt from gemination before $^+/\underset{\sim}{i}/$ and $^+/\underset{\sim}{u}/$. This is understandable because $^+/r/$ is the weakest first contact element before vocalic glides after short vowels in Germanic (not counting diphthongal offglides, which are even weaker and are thus a fortiori exempt from gemination). Contacts of the structure $/r.\underset{\sim}{V}/$ were thus preserved, with an important consequence: whereas the vocalic glides were lost in cases of gemination (i.e. as second elements of medial syllable heads) first in Old English, then in Old High German, and in Low German only after the Old Saxon period, they persisted after $/r/$ – even in Old English, where they were otherwise lost the earliest and without exception.

(77)   OE *settan, scieppan, cynnes, helle-*; but *ferian, gierwan*

In the latter two forms, the glides survive as onsets.

(78)   $^+set.t\underset{\sim}{i}an > set.tan$; but *fer.$\underset{\sim}{i}$an, gier.$\underset{\sim}{u}$an*

In German, the glides survive in a number of examples through Middle High German and are then even strengthened into plosives.

(79)   $^+far.\underset{\sim}{i}o > ver.\underset{\sim}{i}e >$ *Ferge* 'ferryman'
       $^+scar.\underset{\sim}{i}o > scher.\underset{\sim}{i}e >$ *Scherge* 'myrmidon'
       $^+gar.\underset{\sim}{u}\underset{\sim}{i}an > ger.\underset{\sim}{u}en >$ *gerben* 'to prepare
                                    (leather), tan'

Whereas before vocalic glides all consonants with the Consonantal Strength of $^+/1/$ or more are geminated, only the voiceless plosives are affected before liquids. This differential treatment is understandable in light of the Contact Law and the Diachronic Maxim: contacts with liquids as second elements are inherently better than those with vowels (vocalic glides), because liquids are stronger than vowels, and contacts are the better, the stronger their second element is. Therefore, the pressure to change such contacts is a priori weaker, and as long as the first contact element is relatively weak the pressure may not suffice at all. Yet for the very worst clusters of this sort, those with a voiceless plosive as first element, the pressure was strong enough to effect the change. But already the weaker variety of plosives, $^+/b \, d \, g/$, are exempt from gemination, as the Old High German examples in (74.b) show. Needless to say, the same also holds for all the weaker consonants.

One may ask, of course, why West Germanic changed its worst contacts by gemination rather than simply by resyllabication:

(80)   $-\breve{V}C^\$RV\text{-} \, > \, -\breve{V}^\$CRV\text{-}$ (?)

In fact, we did ask ourselves this question and found the answer in the Weight Law, (45): resyllabication as in (80) would be contrary to the Weight Law because the target structures would be less preferred than the source structures in terms of the Weight Law. Gemination satisfies both the Contact Law and the Weight Law, but it does so at the expense of the Head Law. However, since the resulting complex syllable heads are the best possible ones, considering the weakness of their second elements, the process understandably got away with it.

Vincent (1973), suspecting that gemination was an

ordinary sort of sound change like, e.g., umlaut but without realizing its motivation, supports our interpretation by emphasizing the structural parallelism between the West Germanic and the Italian gemination.

(81)   **Gemination in Italian**

|   |   | Latin | Italian |   |
|---|---|---|---|---|
| (a) | $C^\$\underset{\sim}{i}$ | sapiat | sappia | 'he knows (subj.)' |
|   |   | cufia | cuffia | 'bonnet' |
|   |   | radium | raggio | 'ray' |
|   |   | vindemia | vendemmia | 'grape harvest' |
| (b) | $r^\$\underset{\frown}{i}$ | morio | muoio | 'I die' |
| (c) | $C^\$\underset{\sim}{u}$ | futuo | fotto | 'I fornicate' |
|   |   | habui | ebbe | 'I had' |
|   |   | ianuarius | gennaio | 'January' |
|   |   | volui | volli | 'I wanted' |
| (d) | $r^\$\underset{\sim}{u}$ | paruit | parve | 'it seemed' |
| (e) | $C^\$r$ | labrum | labbro | 'lip' |
|   |   | febrem | febbre | 'fever' |
|   |   | Africa | Affrica | 'Africa' |
| (f) | $C^\$l$ | oc(u)lus | occhio | 'eye' |
|   |   | fib(u)la | fibbia | 'buckle' |
|   |   | $^+$duplus | doppio | 'double' |
|   |   | teg(u)la | tegghia | 'baking pan' |

Note in particular the special treatment of /r/. Gemination occurs neither with /r.i̯/ nor with /r.u̯/. Instead, /r/ is lost from its coda before /i̯/, while in the cluster /r.u̯/ the second element is strengthened into a fricative, which allows /r/ to survive in the improved contact /r.v/.

It is easy to misinterpret gemination as progressive assimilation in those cases where the second element of the original contact is subsequently lost, as happened in Old English.

(82)     $^{+}set.\underset{\phantom{.}}{i}an > set.tan$ by progressive assimilation?

The regular preservation of the vocalic glide in Old Saxon (*settian*, etc.) already teaches us that this interpretation is wrong and that the correct interpretation is one assuming two steps, first gemination and then loss of the glides in accordance with the Law of Initials, Old English not permitting complex syllable heads with /i̯/ word-initially.

(83)     $^{+}sat.\underset{\phantom{.}}{i}an > ^{+}set.t\underset{\phantom{.}}{i}an > set.tan$ in Old English

The preservation of the glides in Italian once again shows that gemination is the correct assumption. Pāli was a difficult case because not only glides, but also liquids, and even nasals were lost in the process. Earlier authors therefore assumed progressive assimilation, but Murray (1982) has shown that even for Pāli, gemination with subsequent syllable head simplification in accordance with the Law of Initials is the correct interpretation: Pāli does not allow resonants as second elements of syllable heads word-initially either (or any complex syllable heads, for that matter). Murray was also the first to observe that the assumption of progressive assimilation would contradict the Progressive Assimilation Law (59).

If it is true that changes of the kind $A^{\$}B > A^{\$}A$, where A is stronger than B, are never the result of progressive assimilation, but always of gemination plus syllable head simplification, $A^{\$}B > A^{\$}AB > A^{\$}A$, then new light (or new darkness) falls on certain changes assumed for the pre-history of Proto-Germanic, though often with reservations concerning the value of the evidential etymologies. Clusters of (the reflexes of Proto-Indo-European) plosives and $^{+}/n/$, at least those occurring in positions where Verner's Law would be in effect, are assumed to have changed into geminate plosives by progressive assimilation, though not without exceptions (which may, however, be due to later analogical leveling, at least in part). I quote Prokosch 1939: 70.

(84)  pn' > pp: IE kup-nā́- (OSl. kypéti) Go. *huppōn, ON hoppa, NHG hüpfen

tn' > tt: IE snit-nó- (Go. sneiþan, etc.) MHG snitzen 'whittle' (intensive formation)

dn' > tt: IE (s)tud-nó- (L. tundō, Sk. tudáti, Go. stautan, etc.) MHG stutzen 'be startled'

kn' > kk: IE l̥k-nā́- (L. laciō) ON lokka, OE geloccian, OHG locchōn 'entice'

IE feminine suffix -nī̃ (-nyā̃), as in Sk. patnī̃, Gk. πότνια 'mistress', NHG Ricke, fem. of Reh (Gmc. ráiha-; *rignjā̃ > riggia)

gn' > kk: IE lug-nó- (Lith. lùgnas 'pliable', Gk. λύγος 'twig', λύγινος 'pleated') ON lokkr (but lykna 'bend the knees'), OE loc(c), OHG loc 'lock, curl'

IE bhəgnó- (Gk. φώγω) OHG bacchan 'bake'

ghn' > kk: IE ligh-nā́- (Gk. λείχω 'lick', λιχνεύω 'taste', L. linguo, Go. bilaigon 'lick') OE liccian, OHG lecchōn 'lick'

Whatever the correct interpretation of these and similar examples may be (Prokosch as well as other authors cite a number of additional cases),[32] the assumption of progressive assimilation cannot be right. In the absence of a better hypothesis, I propose gemination with head simplification, viz. after the merger of all three series of plosives as voiced plosives before $^{+}$/n/ (probably with Verner's Law in the case of the original tenues) and before a change of the resulting geminates into geminate fortes.

(85)  (a) P.n T.n K.n > b.n d.n g.n

(b) b.n d.n g.n > b.bn d.dn g.gn
(c) b.bn d.dn g.gn > b.b d.d g.g
(d) b.b d.d g.g > p.p t.t k.k

Attractive though it may seem, the assumption of the gemination in (85.b) is not without its own problems. An attack on the contacts $^+$/b.n d.n g.n/ presupposes an analogous attack on all contacts that are worse; at least this is what the Diachronic Maxim tells us. We do find one fairly bad contact, $^+$/m.u̯/, so attacked, indeed without any regard to the position of the accent (Streitberg 1963: § 127.3).

(86)   Gk. minýō, Lat. minuō 'I diminish', minus 'less';
        Goth. minniza 'smaller'
      Skt. tanuḥ, Lat. tenuis 'thin', Gk. tanú-glōssos
        'longtongued'; OIcel. þunnr, OE ðynne, OHG
        dunni 'thin'
      Skt. riṇvati 'makes flow'; Goth., OS, OHG rin-
        nan, OE yrnan 'to flow'
      Skt. hanuḥ 'jaw', Gk. génys 'lower jaw', Lat.
        dentes genuīnī 'molars'; Goth. kinnus, OIcel.
        kinn 'cheek', OE cin, OHG kinni 'chin'
      Skt. dhanvan- 'bow, arch'; OHG tanna 'fir'

These would indeed be bona fide cases of gemination with subsequent loss of the glide according to the Law of Initials, there being no word-initial $^+$/nu̯/ in Germanic. But since no gemination occurs at this early time in those clusters with liquids and vocalic glides that later undergo the West Germanic gemination, the implication would be that those worse contacts did not exist at the time of the gemination (85.b), at least not in accent positions where Verner's Law would take effect. This in turn would mean that the distribution of CR and CR̥R governed by Sievers'

Law did not exist at the time of this gemination. Or else we would have to assume that all geminates caused by liquids and glides (except $^+/nn/$ from $^+/n.\underset{\ }{u}/$) happened to be eliminated by analogical leveling. But then we may have misunderstood the entire problem, so that perhaps neither progressive assimilation nor gemination need be assumed as a solution for the material of the sort in (84).


# A Catalog for Syllable Contact Changes

Since we have seen two possible remedies for bad syllable contacts, viz. gemination and regressive Strength assimilation, and one that is impossible, viz. progressive Strength assimilation, it would be useful to have a catalog of all the possible remedial change types for bad contacts. I have prepared such a catalog, and I believe it to be complete.[33]

(87) **Types of Syllable Contact Change**
  (1) Tautosyllabication: A . B > . AB
  (2) Gemination: A . B > A . AB
  (3) Calibration
      (a) Coda weakening: A . B > C . B, where C is weaker than A
      (b) Head strengthening: A . B > A . C, where C is stronger than B
  (4) Contact epenthesis: A . B > A . CB, where C is stronger than A
  (5) Strength assimilation
      (a) regressive: A . B > C . B, where the Consonantal Strength of C is less than that of A and greater than or equal to that of B

(b) progressive: A.B > A.C, where the Consonantal Strength of C is less than that of B and greater than or equal to that of A

(6) Contact anaptyxis: A.B > AV.B, where V is a vowel

(7) Contact metathesis: A.B > B.A

Before closing this section, I would like to illustrate all change types on the list, except for gemination, which has already been sufficiently exemplified.

(88)   **Tautosyllabication in Icelandic**

$$\text{(a)} \quad -\breve{V} \begin{Bmatrix} p \\ t \\ k \\ s \end{Bmatrix} \$ \begin{Bmatrix} i \\ \underset{\sim}{u} \\ r \end{Bmatrix} V- \; > \; -\acute{V} \$ \begin{Bmatrix} p \\ t \\ k \\ s \end{Bmatrix} \begin{Bmatrix} i \\ \underset{\sim}{u} \\ r \end{Bmatrix} V-$$

(b)  *vit.ni* 'witness'            BUT   *vī̄.trir* 'wise (nom. pl.)'
     *ep.li* 'apple'                      *lāū.sra* 'loose (gen. pl.)'
     *vis.na* 'to wither'                 *vō̄.kva* 'to water'
     *ek.la* 'to lack'                    *skō̄.pra* 'to roll'
     *ef.ja* 'mud'                        *vē.kja* 'to waken'
     *styð.ja* 'to support'               *flȳ.tja* 'to carry'
     *sel.ja* 'to deliver'                *sē.tja* 'to set'

Icelandic, in contrast with Early West Gemanic, had open syllable lengthening. Therefore, the resyllabication did not create violations of the Weight Law in Icelandic. Furthermore, resyllabication affected only intervocalic contacts of one of the four strongest speech sounds followed by one of the three weakest. Consequently, the resulting complex syllable heads would be the very best ones in terms of the Head Law.

It is interesting to note the prosodic parallelism between gemination on the one hand and resyllabication with open syllable lengthening on the other: in both change types the prosodic length of the first syllable is left untouched.

(89)

$$\text{PGmc. } s\overset{\wedge}{a}\overset{\wedge}{t}.i\underset{\sim}{a}n > \begin{cases} \text{WGmc. } s\overset{\wedge}{e}\,t.t\underset{\sim}{i}an \\ \text{Icel. } \quad s\,e\,e\,.t\underset{\sim}{i}a \\ \qquad\qquad \underset{\vee}{\vee} \end{cases}$$

This may be an important consideration – over and above the Weight Law – in a language with prosodic length, such as Early West Germanic undoubtedly was. In Icelandic, by contrast, the change could take place precisely because prosodic length had been eliminated by open syllable lengthening.

Examples of calibration, viz. of coda weakening, have already been provided in the discussion of the Head Law; I am referring to those cases in (37), (38), and (40) where, in a contact A.B, the Strength of A does not exceed that of B to begin with but decreases nevertheless, such as *cap.ti.vu* > *cau̯.ti.vo*, *pec.tu* (i.e. /pek.tu/) > *pei̯.to* (37), *al.ma* > *ar.ma* (38), [+]*fat.ke* > *far.ke*, [+]*hal.se* > *har.še* (40). It therefore suffices to illustrate the other direction of calibration, head strengthening. This is done in (90), (91), and (92).

(90) **Calibration in German**

*var.u̯e* > *Far.be* 'color'

*su̯al.u̯e* > *Schwal.be* 'swallow'

Cf. (79) for examples with /i̯/ > /g/.

(91) **Calibration in Italian**

*val.i̯o* > *val.go*  'I am valid'

*dol.i̯o* > *dol.go*  'I hurt'

*sal.i̯o* > *sal.go*  'I mount'

*ten.i̯o* > *teŋ.go*  'I hold'

*ven.i̯o* > *veŋ.go*  'I come'

*pon.i̯o* > *poŋ.go* 'I put'[34]

*cor.vo* > *cor.bo, cor.bac.cio*    'raven'

*ner.vo* > *ner.bo*          'nerve'

*cer.vo* > *cer.bo, cer.biat.to*   'hart, fawn'

*ser.va.re* > *ser.ba.re*       'to keep'

*il.va* > *El.ba*

(92) **Calibration in Pāli**

*kur.van.ti* > ⁺*kur.ban.ti* > ⁺*kurb.ban.ti* >
   *kub.ban.ti* 'they make'

Cf. (56) and the two-mora rule for Middle Indic languages (no rhyme may be heavier than two moras).

(93) **Contact epenthesis**

(a) NHG *Zimmer(n)*,  Goth.  *tim(b)rjan*,  E.
     *timber*

NHG *Eller*, E. *alder*

NHG *Männlein*, Bav. *Mandl*

(b) Span. ⁺*ve.ni.rá* > ⁺*ven.rá* > *ven.drá* '(he)
        will come'

       ⁺*po.ni.rá* > ⁺*pon.rá* > *pon.drá* '(hc)
        will put'

Ital. *si.mi.la* > *sim.la* > *sem.bla*
> *sem.bra* 'it seems'

(94)  **Regressive Strength assimilation in Italian**
*val.rà* > *var.rà*   '(he) will be valid'
*dol.rà* > *dor.rà*   '(he) will hurt'
*sal.rà* > *sar.rà*   '(he) will mount'
*ten.rà* > *ter.rà*   '(he) will hold'
*ven.rà* > *ver.rà*   '(he) will come'
*pon.rà* > *por.rà*   '(he) will put'

Cf. also (64), (65). – Progressive Strength assimilation by
Murray's Law has been illustrated in (60), (61), (62), and
(63), e.g. *cal.da* > *cal.la* (60), $^+kol.nis$ > *col.lis* (61),
$^+ster.n\bar{o}$ > *ster.ro* (62), *mar-nónni* → *mar.rónni* (63). All
examples happen to illustrate total assimilation. But
partial assimilation is also quite common in Strength ad-
justments, e.g. Norwegian and Colloquial German *g.n* >
*ŋ.n* (*Sogne* [sɔŋ.nə], *Agnes* [aŋ.nəs]) and *n.t* > *n.d* between Old and Middle High German (*lan.tes* > *lan.des*
'land (gen.)', *un.tar* > *un.der* 'under').

(95)  **Contact anaptyxis**
OHG *zes.wa* ~ *ze.sa.wa*, Goth. *taihswō* 'right
      (hand)'
E. *ath.lete*, non-standard [æ.θə.li̯it]
Ital. *-is.mu* > *-e.si.mo*
      *a.lis.na* > *lé.si.na* 'awl'
      *fan.tas.ma* > *fan.tà.si.ma* 'phantom'

(96)  **Contact metathesis in German**
$^+a.li.ra$ > *e.li.ra* > *el.ra* > *Er.le* 'alder'

(97)   **Contact metathesis in Spanish dialects**

$^+$*ve.ni.rá* > $^+$*ven.rá* > *ver.ná* '(he) will come'
$^+$*po.ni.rá* > $^+$*pon.rá* > *por.ná* '(he) will put'

(98)   **Contact metathesis in Sidamo**

| | | |
|---|---|---|
| *gud-nónni* | → *gun.dónni* | 'they finished' |
| *hab-némmo* | → *ham.bémmo* | 'we forget' |
| *duk-nánni* | → *duŋ.kánni* | 'they carry' |
| *has-némmo* | → *han.sémmo* | 'we look for' |

The examples in (98) illustrate contacts $/A^\$n/$ with greater Consonantal Strength in A than in $/n/$. Only in these cases does metathesis result. The opposite cases are treated by progressive Strength assimilation, as illustrated in (63).

This completes my illustration of the Contact Law and of the types of syllable contact change. Throughout this section, the discussion focussed on the contacts themselves, namely on their quality as a function of the relative Consonantal Strength of the two speech sounds involved. This may have created the impression that within this theory the quality of a syllabication is to be understood entirely as a matter of speech sounds in contact. A demonstration that this is not the case will be part of the next section, which illustrates complex interactions of some of the preference laws with additional factors.

# Complex applications

Even though my survey of syllable structure change types is long – to my knowledge it is the most comprehensive survey that has ever been produced – it is not complete. When reading in the phonological histories of various languages, one finds surprising syllable structure changes all the time, some of them of miraculous subtlety. I would like to cite one of these miracles. We have seen that complex syllable heads are the more preferred, the sharper the Strength drop from the onset toward the nucleus, as stated in the Head Law, part (c); an obvious cure for disfavored heads is the weakening of consonants on the slope, the part between onset and nucleus, as illustrated in (23). This strikes me as a fairly subtle mechanism, because it only affects the phonic substance of the string to a small degree. To my personal taste, the epitome of elegance in change is reached in those alterations in which the phonic substance is not touched at all but only the order of elements is changed to attain a more preferred structure. Thus, in my opinion metathesis is the most elegant type of contact change. Such elegance may also be attained in slope improvement.

(99)  **Slope metathesis in Spanish**

*pe.rí.cu.lu* > *pe.rí.clu* > *pe.lí.gro* 'danger'
*mi.rá.cu.lu* > *mi.rá.clu* > *mi.lá.gro* 'miracle'
*pa.rá.bo.la* > *pa.rá.bla* > *pa.lá.bra* 'word'

A vaguely similar procedure consists in the shift of a bothersome slope element to a syllabically analogous position where it does less harm, so to speak, viz. from the slope of an unstressed syllable to that of a stressed syllable, in accordance with the following very general "higher order" law.

(100)    All syllabic complexities are less disfavored in stressed syllables than in unstressed syllables.

(101)    **Slope displacement in Italian**

*co.mu.lu* > *co.mlu* (?) > *clo.mu* > *chio.mo* 'hill' (Old Ital.)

*fa.bu.la* > *fa.bla* (?) > *fla.ba* > *fia.ba* 'fairy tale'

*fun.du.la* > *fun.dla* (?) > *flun.da* > *fion.da* 'catapult'

*po.pu.lu* > *pop.lu* > *pop.plu* > *plop.po* > *piop.po* 'poplar'

Finally, I would like to draw attention to the need for a generalization of the Syllable Contact Law. It is a well-known fact that the syllabication of internuclear clusters does not only depend on the quality of the resulting syllable contacts, but also on other factors, chief among them the accentual environment of the clusters. Lutz has shown in recent analyses of Old English syllabication (1985, 1986) that three factors determine the position of the syllable boundary in Old English words:

1. The position of the accent, viz. the question of whether the syllable preceding the cluster is accented or not.
2. The length of the nucleus preceding the cluster.
3. In clusters of three, the Consonantal Strength of the first element of the cluster.

She demonstrates the relevance of each of these factors by comparing divisions of words in which all other possible factors are kept constant. For example, the intervocalic cluster *dr* is divided (*d/r*) 49 times and taken undivided to the next line (*/dr*) 48 times in the entire corpus of approximately 65,000 investigated word divisions. The impression of a random distribution disappears when words with the structure *VdrV* are compared that differ in regard to the position of the accent. Thus, the occurrences of *nǽdrV-* with the accent immediately before the cluster, and those of words such as *wéredre*, *unfulfrémedre* with no accent immediately before the cluster are divided with the following frequencies:

(102)  *nǽdrV-* (´x)     12 *d/r*      1 */dr*
       [xx]´-xx          4 *d/r*     17 */dr*

Evidently an accented first syllable tends more strongly to attract part of the cluster toward itself than an unaccented first syllable, and the resulting difference in syllabication is reflected in the different division ratios.

The intervocalic cluster *þr* is divided (*þ/r*) 108 times and kept together (*/þr*) 181 times. When looking at individual words of the same accentual pattern but with different nuclear length immediately before the cluster, one finds different ratios:

(103)  (-)*hwǽþre* (´x)      5 *þ/r*       5 */þr*
       (-)*brōþrV-* (´x)    22 *þ/r*     104 */þr*

Evidently a syllable with a long nucleus tends less strongly to attract part of the cluster to itself than does a syllable with a short nucleus.

For intervocalic clusters of three that end in *dr*, the total ratios are as follows (postvocalic *dr* is repeated for comparison):

| (104) | 49 | $Vd/r$ | 48 | $V/dr$ | $\sim$ | $1:1$ |
|---|---|---|---|---|---|---|
| | 19 | $rd/r$ | 30 | $r/dr$ | $\sim$ | $1:1,5$ |
| | 23 | $ld/r$ | 134 | $l/dr$ | $\sim$ | $1:6$ |
| | 26 | $nd/r$ | 304 | $n/dr$ | $\sim$ | $1:12$ |
| | 3 | $dd/r$ | 71 | $d/dr$ | $\sim$ | $1:24$ |

Evidently a first syllable tends the less to attract a second cluster constant, the stronger the first consonant of the cluster is.[35]

For Contemporary Standard German I have intuitions corresponding to those which have to be assumed for the Old English scribes on the evidence of their gradient word divisions. For example, in words of the pattern $-\acute{V}(C)sP\partial$-, where $P$ is a voiceless plosive,[36] the syllabication is without any doubt $\acute{V}s.P\partial$ for lax (and therefore short) vowels: *Wes.pe* 'wasp', *Wes.te* 'vest', *Bas.ke* 'Basque'. Uncertainty begins after tense (and therefore long) vowels and after diphthongs: is the correct syllabication *Bies.ter* or *Bie.ster* 'beasts', *Meis.ter* or *Mei.ster* 'master'? And in *Förster* 'forester', *erster* (with long *e*) 'first', *Elster* 'magpie', *Wahlster* (with long *a*, a name), *Münster* 'minster', *schönster* (with long *ö*) 'most beautiful', *Äxte* 'axes', I incline increasingly toward the division $-VC.sP\partial$-, even though the division $-VCs.P\partial$- also appears possible in every single case. As for the role of accentuation, I feel that while *monás.tisch* 'monastic' is the only possible syllabication, *Mona.stérium* 'monastery' appears possible alongside *Monas.térium*.

These observations seem to warrant the following generalization. First we divide complex nuclei, viz. long vowels and narrowing diphthongs, into a peak and a satellite: $\bar{V} = \underset{\shortmid}{V}V$ (with identical one-mora vowels), $V\underline{V} = \underset{\shortmid}{V}V$ (with different one-mora vowels). The resulting classification of cluster environments is the following: (a) according to the distance from the preceding peak –

$VC_1C_2$ vs. $VXC_1C_2$ –, which can be described in terms of length; (b) according to the kinds of segment in X – vowel, glide, $r$, $l$, etc. –, which can be captured in terms of Consonantal Strength. Next we define the concept of attractiveness for rhymes of syllables.

(105)   **Attractiveness of Rhymes**
        A rhyme is the more attractive: (a) the more heavily its syllable is accented relative to the following syllable, (b) the shorter it is, and (c) the less the Consonantal Strength of its elements is, especially towards its offset.

With this concept, Lutz's discovery for Old English can be generalized into a universal preference law:

(106)   **Lutz's Law**
        Heterosyllabication of an internuclear cluster is the more preferred, the more attractive the rhyme of that syllable is which would remain of the first syllable if the cluster were tautosyllabicated in the second syllable.

For example, heterosyllabication of *kr* would be more preferred in *ák.ros* than in *ak.rós* because the rhyme of the first syllable is more attractive in *á.kros* than in *a.krós*; and this would be so because *a* would be more heavily accented in *á.kros* than in *a.krós*. Heterosyllabication of the cluster would also be more preferred in *ák.ros* than in *ā̆k.ros* – and likewise in *ak.rós* compared to *āk.rós* – because the rhyme of *a* in *a.kros* is shorter than that of *ā* ($= \underset{\shortmid}{a}a$) in *ā.kros*. And again heterosyllabication would be more preferred in *āk.ros* than in *alk.ros* because the Consonantal Strength of the second *a* in $\underset{\shortmid}{a}a$*.kros* would be less than that of *l* in *al.kros*. Heterosyllabication of *kr* would be considerably better in *álk.ros* than in, say, *āŋk.rós* because of a combination of all three factors which make the rhyme of the first syllable in *ál.kros* much more attractive than that in *āŋ.krós*.

Lutz's Law only compares syllable contacts to their environment in the first syllable. But it is easy to see that the second syllable has a rather similar influence on the syllabication of internuclear clusters.

First, the effect of accent placement is rather symmetrical: an accented syllable exerts a greater attraction also on *preceding* cluster elements than does an unaccented one. I already mentioned the possibility of a syllabication -*V.stV*- in German simplicia only with accented second syllables. I also find it much easier to say *Ma.gnét* rather than *Á.gnes*; *Ágnes* tends to become *Á*[ŋ].*nes* (for many Northern speakers *Á*[x].*nes*), namely via a hypothetical /ág.nəs/ (/áɣ.nəs/ for Northern speakers), which is itself excluded because of final devoicing.

That the length of the body of the second syllable – the counterpart of the length of the rhyme of first syllables – plays a role is seen in pairs such as *Estin* vs. *estnisch* /ēstɪn, ēstnɪʃ/ 'Estonian (fem.noun vs. adj.)'. The syllabications */ēst.ɪn/, /ēst.nɪʃ/ would leave a shorter body in the first example than in the second. This is reflected in the actual syllabications /ēs.tɪn, ēst.nɪʃ/.

But the Consonantal Strength of the head elements is also a factor. Thus, even though the length of the bodies of both *ma* and *ro* is the same, *Asthma* is /ást.ma/, whereas *Astro*- (in *Astrophysik*) is /ás.tro-/. An objection might be that this is an effect of the Law of Initials, Standard German having word-initial /tr/ but not /tm, tn/. But the same differentiation may be found where both head clusters are tolerated word-initially. For example, if the stems *asp*- and *bask*- were subjected to derivation on the model of *Estin, estnisch*, the results would be *As.pin* but *asp.nisch*, and *Bas.kin* but *bask.nisch*, even though both / pn / and / kn / occur word-initially, the former in a well-established loan-word (*Pneu, pneumatisch*), the latter in native words (*Knie*). In Gothic, all intervocalic consonant clusters, of whatever length, are divided in such a way that only the final consonant is taken to the second syllable – the sole exception being the case of obstruent plus liquid. Nevertheless, several of the clusters thus divided are quite normal in the word-initial position. For example, *þrafs/tei* (*gaþrafs/tidedeina, gaþrafs/tein*) 'comfort' testifies to a syllabication -*Vfs.tV*-; neverless, word-initial / st / is normal in this language, cf. *standan* 'stand', *stains* 'stone', and many others.

I would therefore like to generalize Lutz's Law into a more general preference law that accommodates the observed symmetry. I begin with definitions of the required concepts.

(107) **Attractiveness of Bodies**
A body is the more attractive: (a) the more heavily its syllable is accented relative to the preceding syllable, (b) the shorter it is, and (c) the less the Consonantal Strength of its elements is, especially towards its onset.

Rather than formulate a second-syllable counterpart of Lutz's Law, I would like to introduce one further concept, thus preparing the way for a generalization that covers both cases and integrates them with the Contact Law.

(108) **Quality of Contact Embedding**
A syllable contact A$^\$$B is the better embedded, the more attractive the rhyme of the first syllable would be if the cluster AB were tautosyllabicated in the second syllable, and the more attractive the

body of the second syllable would be if the cluster AB were tautosyllabicated in the first syllable.

(109)   **General Syllabication Law**
A syllabication is the more preferred: (a) the better[37] the resulting syllable contact is and (b) the better that syllable contact is embedded.

# Concluding Remarks

I would like to conclude my discussion of the preference laws for syllable structure with a few general remarks.

1. The preference laws express partially conflicting tendencies. For instance, the Contact Law characterizes a syllable contact as the better, the stronger its second element is; by contrast, the Strength Assimilation Law qualifies a syllable contact as the better, the less the Strength of the stronger of the contact elements. I do not consider this a defect of the theory. I mentioned at the beginning that improvement on one parameter can entail deterioration on another. It is impossible to optimize a language system on all parameters at once; there can exist no "optimal" language system as such, but only systems that are optimized on some parameters. The same holds true even within the narrow limits of syllable structure – it is impossible to optimize all syllable structure parameters at once. Even the so-called ideal syllable, CV, with a strong consonant followed by a vowel, is optimal only in isolation; combined with other ideal syllables, it automatically becomes bad in certain positions, viz. by the very strength of its onset, and as such, it becomes subject to local improvements, e.g. weakening, possibly all the way to zero. Evidently, there is no optimal syllable structure, but only syllable structure for which some parameters are optimized.

2. The preference laws for syllable structure determine

the direction of syllable structure change. This is so because all sound changes are local improvements, i.e. improvements on certain parameters, and the relative quality of structures is characterized by the relevant preference laws. It follows that when syllable structure is altered without any resulting syllable structure improvement, or even with a deterioration of syllable structure, the change is not a syllable structure change in the technical sense but a change motivated by some other factor, only incidentally affecting syllable structure. I would like to provide a single, very subtle example of this sort from the history of Italian.

(110)  *aera* > *ai.re* > *a.ria* (*a.re*) 'air'
    *bajula* > +*bai.la* > *ba.lia* /ba.ʎa/ 'nurse'
    *magida* > *mai.da* > *ma.dia* 'kneading trough'
    *pagina* > *pai.na* > *pa.nia* /pa.ɲa/ 'birdlime'

The Contact Law tells us that a metathetic change away from /i̯$C/, where C is stronger than /i̯/, is not a syllable structure improvement. Indeed, the normal direction of change in contact metathesis is in fact the exact opposite, as illustrated in (111).

(111)  Gk. +*katʰár.i̯ō* > *katʰaí.rō* 'I purify'
    +*bán.i̯ō* > *baí.nō* 'I walk'
    +*pʰtʰér.i̯ō* > *pʰtʰeí.rō* 'I ruin'
    +*ktén.i̯ō* > *kteí.nō* 'I slay'
    +*krín.i̯ō* > *krī́.nō* 'I separate'
    +*plún.i̯ō* > *plȳ́.nō* 'I wash'
    Boeot. *kal.Fós*, Homer. *kā.lós* 'beautiful'
    Cor. *xén.Fos*, Homer. *xeî.nos* /ę̂/,
      Cyren. *xẽ.nos* /ę̂/ 'guest'
    Cor. *kór.Fā*, Homer. *koú.rē* /ǫ́/,
      Cret. *kṓ.rā* /ǫ́/ 'girl'

66

Span. *sap.i̯a* > *sai̯.pa* > *se.pa* '(he) knows (subj.)'
   *al.tar.i̯o* > *al.tai̯.ro* > *o.te.ro* 'hill'
   *bas.i̯o* > *bai̯.so* > *be.so* 'kiss'
   *sap.u̯i* > *sau̯.pi* > *su.pe* 'I knew'
   *cǫr.i̯o* > *cǫi̯.ro* 'leather' (Old Span.)

In my interpretation of the Italian change, the motivation is the aversion – evident throughout the entire history of Italian – against narrowing diphthongs. While evidently being very fond of their widening diphthongs /i̯ɛ u̯ɛ i̯ɔ u̯ɔ/ etc., speakers of Italian have always been very skillful in doing away with narrowing diphthongs.

(112)   *fa.bu.la* > *fab.la* > *fau̯.la* > *fo.la* 'fairy tale'
   *Pau.lu* > *Po.lo*
   *Pau.lu* > *Pa.o.lo* > *Pa.vo.lo, Pa.go.lo*

I believe that the metathetic removal of /i̯/ from the diphthong /ai̯/ is simply the greatest triumph of the Italian monophthongal genius.

   3. Finally, I would like to draw attention to the explanatory power of the preference laws. By telling us what sort of syllable structure is universally preferred, they allow us to understand syllable structure restrictions in individual languages as well as types of syllable structure change manifest in the history of individual languages. They are explanatory not in the strong sense of prediction, but in the weak sense of elucidation: knowing them, we do not stand in the dark vis-à-vis individual syllable structure restrictions or changes, but understand them – we recognize their motivation. The preferences are rooted in the human phonetic endowment; the laws are explained (or will be explained, I trust) in a general phonetic theory. Their phonetic foundation at the same time accounts for their universality.

Discovering order in apparent randomness, universality in language-specific details, explanations for what seemed to be just facts to be lived with, appears to me to be genuine progress. Even so, our knowledge is to date merely disparate and fragmented. Yet I am confident that as we follow this course of investigation, we will gain ever more, and more coherent, insights. I believe that the strongest unifying forces in the sound structure of our languages have yet to be found. The greatest discoveries in the theory of linguistic prosody still lie ahead of us.

# Notes

[1] General characterizations of the concept of preference laws have been attempted in Vennemann 1983a, b. Some initial illustration in the domain of syllable structure is contained in a chapter of Vennemann 1986.

[2] It shares this property with Bailey's and Mayerthaler's conception of markedness, cf. e.g. Bailey 1978 and Mayerthaler 1982.

[3] The optimal syllable structure, as is well known, is CV.CV.CV etc., with alternating single consonants and vowels. Diphthongs deviate from this structure by being tautosyllabic VV sequences. That apocopation and syncopation worsen syllable structure can be seen most easily by applying them to the optimal pattern: CV.CV.CV̱ > CV.CVC, with a less preferred CVC syllable; CV.CV̱.CV > CV.CCV or > CVC.CV, with a less preferred CCV or CVC syllable.

[4] My understanding of language change has benefited from the collaboration with Robert W. Murray over a number of years; cf. Murray and Vennemann 1982, 1983, Murray 1982 and his doctoral dissertation. Murray is, of course, not responsible for any specification, formulation, or exemplification given in this lecture.

[5] The concept of language-specific normalcy has been developed and compared to that of universal naturalness by Wolfgang Ullrich Wurzel, most recently as morphological system adequacy in Wurzel 1984: 75–80.

[6] I have pointed out a number of problems of syllabic phonologies in Vennemann MSa. But I believe that the preference laws remain valid even if syllable structure itself turns out merely to be epiphenomenal in a more general phonological theory. In the limiting case of languages without syllable structure, such as Gokana, if Hyman (1985: 27) is right, the laws would simply not be applicable.

[7] It is evident that all these functions should be indexed with the name of the language system under study, e.g. with a subscript "E" if "E" is the name of the system of some variety of English. I will omit this index in the interest of brevity.

[8] E.g., the two syllables of the English word *apron* are assigned the bases /ei/ and /prn/, respectively. – I am assuming, for

69

this and the following illustrations, a phonological theory for English which recognizes nuclear ("syllabic") resonants.

[9] The nucleus function assigns the first syllable of *apron* the nucleus /e/ (or the entire diphthong /ei/, in some theories), its second syllable the nucleus $^3$/n/. [The superscript number indicates the position where a sub-sequence begins within its sequence; the position number 1 is usually omitted.] A conventional way of marking nuclei is by means of a vertical stroke under the nuclear position, e.g. /ẹi/ and /prn̦/. However, the stroke is usually omitted under nuclear vowels, and in cases of diphthongs it is usually the non-nuclear component that is marked, viz. by means of a subscript half-moon, e.g. /eị/. – Chief among the moric properties of syllables is nuclear length in languages such as Old English, Latin, and Japanese. For example, the first syllables of the Latin words *malum* 'evil' and *malum* 'apple' [the latter spelled *mālum* in modern dictionaries] have the same base, /ma/, but π assigns the former nuclear shortness, the latter nuclear length. In some theories nuclear length is represented as bisegmentality, e.g. /maa/. The tone function is empty for standard English systems but not, e.g., for Chinese ones. – Syllable cut properties are recognized for Standard German unreduced syllables, viz. **smooth cut** and **abrupt cut**. Smoothly cut syllables have tense vowels (long when accented) and may be closed or open. Abruptly cut syllables have lax vowels (always short) and must be closed, either basically or prosodically, namely by ambisyllabicity. Cf. Vennemann MSb and the references given there.

[10] Unless Hockett (1955: 57–59) is right in assuming an "onset type" of language with syllables whose bases may contain only a head consonant. Cf. also Hoard 1978.

[11] This is even true for standard varieties of English if nuclear consonants are assumed for unstressed syllables, compare *apron* /ei.prn̦/ to *lantern* /læn.trn̦/; both /ei.prn̦/ and /læn.trn̦/ are phonologically possible (and /ei.pṛn/ is real in some varieties), and the choice is not free. Thus /rn̦/ and /ṛn/ stand in opposition, i.e., the position of nuclearity is contrastive in such a system (under such a theory).

[12] For example, the one syllable of the English word *sprint* with its base /sprɪnt/ and nucleus $^4$/ɪ/ has the head /spr/, the coda $^5$/nt/, the body /sprɪ/, the rhyme $^4$/ɪnt/, and the shell

/spr□nt/, i.e. /spr/ ∪ $^5$/nt/. – The representation of the shell shows the importance of the position numbers: the shell is not, of course, /sprnt/, which would be /spr/ ∪ $^4$/nt/.

[13] Thus, the one syllable of the English word *ask* is naked and closed, that of *spa* is covered and open.

[14] For instance, in Latin the first syllable of *malum* 'evil' is light because it is open (/ma.lum/) and its nucleus is short (cf. above, fn. 9); that of *malum* 'apple' is heavy because of the length of its nucleus, even though it is open (/ma.lum/ or, with marked length, /mā.lum/ or /maa.lum/), and that of *malleus* 'hammer' (/mal.le.us/) is heavy because it is closed. In Latin this prosodic distinction is crucial for accent placement; in polysyllables the accent goes on the penult if it is heavy, otherwise on the antepenult: *laudátus* 'praised' (with nuclear length on the penult), *moléstus* 'burdened' (with a closed penult, /mo.les.tus/), but *dóminus* 'lord', *málleus* 'hammer', *íntegrum* 'whole (neut.sg.nom./acc.)', each with nuclear shortness in the open penult. The prosodic distinction is also crucial in Latin poetry, where in many verse positions one heavy syllable and two light syllables are metrically equivalent.

[15] Thus, if *malum* 'evil' and *malum* 'apple' are represented as /ma.lum/ vs. /maa.lum/ (cf. above, fn. 9), the cardinality of the rhymes of their first syllables, $^2$/a/ and $^2$/aa/, and therefore the number of moras of their first syllables, is one and two, respectively.

[16] E.g., the onset and offset of the one syllable of the English word *sprint* with its basis /sprɪnt/ are /s/ and $^6$/t/, respectively. Those of *sprints* would be /s/ (= $^1$/s/) and $^7$/s/ – which shows, once again, the importance of the position numbers.

[17] This is so because the word phonological part of a grammar can be developed without any reference to non-phonological properties of words.

[18] Consider the Spanish words *tomo* '(I) take' and *tomó* '(he) took'. They have the same foundation properties, viz. they both contain the same sequence of syllables, one with the basis /to/ and nucleus $^2$/o/, the other with the basis /mo/ and nucleus $^2$/o/. The only phonological difference is their accentual properties: *tomo* '(I) take' is accented on the first syllable, *tomó* '(he) took' on the second. The two words have identical FO values but different Π values. This particular Π value, the

"word accent", determines where the sentence accent is placed whenever the word is accented within sentences (including the one-word sentences we use to demonstrate "word accent"). It may also determine certain properties in the foundation that synchronically or diachronically derive from sentence accentuation, such as length, vowel reduction, and syllabication. – Whereas in Chinese a polysyllabic word receives its tones from its foundation, viz. from the individual syllables that enter into it, in Mende, a Mande language of Sierra Leone, tone, according to Leben 1978: 186, seems to be a property of entire words, at least in a large number of regular cases. The five main tone patterns are (with H or ´ for 'high tone' and L or ` for 'low tone'): H, L, HL, LH, and LHL. These may all occur on a single syllable, in which case the tone sequences are compressed into complex tones: HL becomes a falling tone (´ ` → ˆ), LH a rising tone (` ´ → ˇ), and LHL a circumflex or rising-plus-falling tone (` ´ ` → ᵕ). On polysyllables the tones are matched with the individual syllables starting with the first one; if there are not enough syllables, the remaining tones are compressed, and if there are not enough tones, the last tone is spread to the end of the word. Thus, the three words *mbă* 'rice', *fàndé* 'cotton', and *ndàvúlá* 'sling' would all have the same word tone pattern LH, and the three words *mbâ* 'compassion', *nyàhâ* 'woman', and *nìkílì* 'groundnut' the same word tone pattern LHL. To this extent it seems adequate to say that Mende tonal patterns are word prosodies rather than prosodies of individual syllables. – In Turkish, where the backness and roundness values of vowels in sequences of suffixes are determined by the values of the last stem vowel in all the most ordinary words, the harmonic distribution of these feature values is recognizably a word prosody.

[19] I usually use "$" rather than "." to mark syllable breaks where the latter would not be clear or conspicuous enough, i.e. especially in the formulation of rules.

[20] Since the two Spanish words *tomo* '(I) take' and *tomó* '(he) took' have the same foundation (cf. above, fn. 18), they also have the same word basis, viz. /tomo/, resulting from the concatenation of the individual syllable bases /to/ and /mo/.

[21] Cf. above, fn. 9.

[22] Assuming for the sake of illustration that in Classical Greek

all nasals are of equal Strength, all plosives are of equal Strength, plosives are stronger than nasals, and nasals stronger than vowels, then the first syllables of the words *mnḗmē* 'remembrance' and *pterón* 'feather' illustrate weakly but not strongly monotonic heads and bodies, and that of the word *pnéō* '(I) blow' a strongly monotonic head and body. If analogous assumptions are made for English, then the word *apt* illustrates a weakly but not strongly monotonic coda and rhyme while the word *ant* illustrates a strongly monotonic coda and rhyme. The English word *sprints*, under the assumption that fricatives are weaker than plosives, illustrates a non-monotonic head, body, coda, and rhyme.

23  Under the assumptions made above in fn. 22, all the syllables of the Greek words *mnḗmē* 'remembrance' and *pterón* 'feather' and the one syllable of the English word *apt* are weakly monotonic, while the two syllables of *pnéō* '(I) blow' and the one syllable of *ant* are strongly monotonic.

24  Still under the same assumptions, the two syllables of *pnéō* and the one syllable of *ant* are core syllables, and whereas the syllable of *sprints* is not monotonic at all, that of *print*, whose basis is contained in that of *sprints*, is strongly monotonic and thus another example of a core syllable.

25  Using the last example of the preceding footnote, we can identify /prɪnt/ as the core of the syllable of *sprints* (as well as that of *print*, incidentally, because the core of a core syllable is identical to its base). More precisely speaking, the core of a syllable is the largest portion of its base that *after renumbering such that its initial position number is one* could be the basis of a core syllable. Thus, the cores of *skill* and *sprints* are $^2$/kɪl/ and $^2$/prɪnt/ because they are the largest portions of /skɪl/ and /sprɪnts/ that, as /kɪl/ and /prɪnt/, are the bases of possible and, indeed, real core syllables of English.

26  Thus, one may produce good arguments for the assumption that the Standard German "diphthongs" /aɪ aʊ ɔʏ/ are entirely nuclear. If the arguments are accepted, then there is the rhyme constraint that /r/ may not be the onset of a coda after a "diphthongal" nucleus, while (a) this is not so for any true monophthongal nucleus and (b) any stronger consonant than /r/ may be the onset of a coda after a "diphthongal" nucleus, cf. Vennemann MSa; and that may reflect a universal preference for rhymes.

[27] See the examples in (19) and (20) below.

[28] Not being a Romance scholar I have relied, for all Italian examples, on Rohlfs 1972, Mańczak 1978, Genot 1979, and Tekavčić 1980, all of which I have freely borrowed from without giving credit for individual examples. I beg forgiveness for not distinguishing systematically between attested and inferred Vulgar Latin examples; while this may be abhorrent to some Romanists, I feel it is innocuous for my modest purpose of demonstrating by illustration while simplifying the presentation by the avoidance of various letter types. Needless to say, my nonchalance in these matters, as well as any errors of fact or interpretation, should not be suspected of deriving from my sources. For the Latin and Germanic examples I have relied on various traditional sources that happened to be at hand.

[29] That is to say that a non-final syllable ending in /s/ before a plosive counts metrically as heavy (it also does for the accent rule, cf. /mo.lés.tus/, */mó.le.stus/), whereas a *final* open syllable with a short vowel metrically counts as light, even if the following word begins with /s/ plus plosive; cf. Zirin 1970: 41.

[30] Cf. fn. 29 above.

[31] The clusters CR were intervocalic throughout in the earlier history of these languages; cf. the paradigm forms OE *æpples* (gen. sg.), *fugles*, later changed to *fugoles* on the analogy of the nominative and accusative *fugol* 'fowl'; OHG *fogales* had ousted ⁺*fogles* by the time of the earliest records. Gothic has dat. pl. *fuglam*. The separated clusters derive from word-final -VCRV via apocope, nuclearization of R, and anaptyxis: ⁺-VCRV > ⁺-VCR > ⁺-VCR̩ > -VCVR.

[32] The most recent treatment is Lühr 1980.

[33] Tom Shannon has pointed out to me that nothing in my definitions prevents the interpretation of hiatus as (the limiting case of) syllable contact and that this particular kind of contact, V$V, is subject to changes not covered by (87). Namely, we frequently find *denuclearization*, V$V > V̯V or > VV̯ (the direction usually depending on the relative narrowness of the abutting vowels), as well as *elision*, i.e. loss of one of the two vowels. He is, of course, right, and these remedial measures should be added to the catalog, at least as a footnote. As a matter of fact, we also find *contraction* of two vowels into one

long vowel, a measure which should be added to the list, too. Finally, there is *glide insertion*, as exemplified in (7) and (8) in our illustration of the Head Law; but that could be subsumed under contact epenthesis, viz. by adding the condition "and B" at the end of (87.4), provided that glides of all sorts as well as the glottal stop are understood as having greater Consonantal Strength than nuclear vowels, which is, indeed, a most common assumption.

[34] Se non è vero, è ben trovato. It is not true, as Yakov Malkiel kindly reminded me after hearing this lecture, and I could have remembered myself, knowing as I do his brilliant 1968 article. The regular development of *li̯* and *ni̯* would be a (geminate) palatalized lateral or nasal respectively, i.e. *ʎ(ʎ)*, *ñ(ñ)*, e.g. *pa.le.a* > *⁺pa.li.a* > *⁺pal.i̯a* > *⁺pal.li̯a* > *⁺paʎ.ʎa* > *pa.ʎa*, i.e. *paglia* 'straw', *vi.ne.a* > *⁺vi.ni.a* > *⁺vin.i̯a* > *⁺vin.ni̯a* > *⁺viñ.ña* > *vi.ña*, i.e. *vigna* 'vinyard', cf. Rohlfs 1972: 460–464. The attested forms *valgo* (*\*vaglio*), *pongo* (*\*pogno*), etc. can therefore only be of analogical origin; cf. e.g. Tekavčić 1980: 279.

[35] I have shown in a forthcoming paper (MSc) that Gothic scribes possessed a similar sensitivity to the environment of a given cluster: While clusters of obstruent (*p, t, k, b, d, g, þ*) plus liquid (*r, l*) are regularly taken to the second line in one group of manuscripts (Codex Argenteus, Codex Ambrosianus A), the same is true for another group of manuscripts (Codex Ambrosianus B, *Skeireins*, Nehemiah fragment) only if the cluster is preceded by a consonant (*-VC/OLV-*), while after vowels the practice is the following: After short vowels the cluster is divided (*-VO/LV-*), and after long vowels (and diphthongs) both divided and undivided cases occur in apparently free variation (*-V̄O/LV-*, *-V̄/OLV-*). I interpret the two different division procedures as evidence for two varieties of Gothic, of which the latter reflects more closely the Proto-Germanic syllabication, while the former shows a resyllabication – the *Correptio Gotica* or *Argentea* – comparable to the *Correptio Attica* described in Allen 1973: 210ff. – Also Proto-Germanic itself is a case in point: While all clusters of obstruent plus resonant are divided after short vowels of accented syllables (*-VO.RV-*), after long vowels (and diphthongs) and after consonants of accented syllables they belong entirely to the following syllable, where further-

more the resonant is nuclearized $(-\bar{V}.OR.(R)V-,$
$-VC.OR.(R)V-)$ according to Sievers' Law (cf. the most recent demonstration in Murray 1986).

[36] Since clusters with *dr* are not problematical in German, and *þ*
– and thus *þr* – does not occur in that language, I use clusters
of *s* plus plosive. Even though clusters with *s* are known to be
special in many regards, they are well-suited for the purpose
of demonstrating the dependence of syllabication on environments. Lutz (1986: 208) has shown this for Old English. There
the ratio of *s/t* vs. */st* divisions depends on the preceding
speech sounds as follows:

|            | *s/t* | */st* |   |        |
|------------|-------|-------|---|--------|
| -$\acute{V}$st- | 108   | 9     | ~ | 12:1   |
| -$\grave{V}$st- | 87    | 25    | ~ | 3.5:1  |
| -$\acute{V}$rst- | 25    | 80    | ~ | 1:3    |
| -$\acute{V}$Cst- $(C \neq r)$ | 6 | 119 | ~ | 1:20   |

And after short vowels, the ratio depends on the accent, viz.
´x vs. ´xx, as follows:

|         | *s/t* | */st* |   |       |
|---------|-------|-------|---|-------|
| -$\acute{V}$st- | 108   | 9     | ~ | 12:1  |
| -$V$st-  | 67    | 13    | ~ | 5:1   |

Adducing my intuitions for *sP* clusters is therefore to the
point.

[37] "Better" is brief for 'more preferred according to the Syllable
Contact Law'.

# Abbreviations

| | |
|---|---|
| abl. | ablative |
| acc. | accusative |
| adj. | adjective |
| And. | Andalusian |
| Bav. | Bavarian |
| Boeot. | Boeotian |
| Cor. | Corinthian |
| Cors. | Corsican |
| Cret. | Cretan |
| Cyren. | Cyrenaean |
| dat. | dative |
| dem. | demonstrative |
| dial. | dialect(al) |
| E. | English |
| fem. | feminine |
| Fr. | French |
| G. | German |
| gen. | genitive |
| Gk. | Greek |
| Gmc. | Germanic |
| Goth., Go. | Gothic |
| Homer. | Homeric |
| IE | (Proto-)Indo-European |
| ind. | indicative |
| instr. | instrumental |
| Ital. | Italian |
| Lat., L. | Latin |
| Lesb. | Lesbian |
| Lith. | Lithuanian |
| masc. | masculine |
| MHG | Middle High German |
| NHG | New High German |
| nom. | nominative |
| OCS | Old Church Slavic |
| OE | Old English |
| OFr. | Old French |
| OFris. | Old Frisian |
| OHG | Old High German |
| OIcel. | Old Icelandic |

| | |
|---|---|
| OIr. | Old Irish |
| ON | Old Norse |
| OS | Old Saxon |
| OSl. | Old Slavic |
| pers. | person |
| PGmc. | Proto-Germanic |
| pl. | plural |
| pron. | pronoun |
| sg. | singular |
| Skt., Sk. | Sanskrit |
| Sic. | Sicilian |
| Span. | Spanish |
| subj. | subjunctive |
| WGmc. | West Germanic |

# Special Symbols

| | |
|---|---|
| $ (or ".") | syllable boundary |
| + | a reconstructed form |
| * | an incorrect form (in quotations: a reconstructed form) |
| > | 'was changed diachronically into' |
| → | 'is changed morphophonemically into' |
| / / | phonological transcription |
| [ ] | narrow ("phonetic") transcription |

# References

Allen, W. Sidney (1973). *Accent and rhythm*. Cambridge: Cambridge University Press.

Bailey, Charles-James (1978). *Gradience in English syllabization and a revised concept of marked syllabization*. Bloomington, Indiana: Indiana University Linguistics Club.

Bell, Alan (1978). Syllabic consonants. In Joseph H. Greenberg (ed.), *Universals of human language,* vol. 2: *Phonology*, 153–201. Stanford: Stanford University Press.

Geiger, Wilhelm (1916). *Pāli Literatur und Sprache* ( = *Grundriß der Indo-Arischen Philologie und Altertumskunde* 1.7). Straßburg: Karl J. Trübner. [English translation by Batakrishna Gosh, *Pāli literature and language*, 2nd ed., Delhi: Oriental Books Reprint Corporation, 1968.]

Genot, Gérard (1979). *Notes de linguistique italienne: 1 – Phonologie diachronique*. Université de Nanterre.

Grammont, Maurice (1950). *Traité de phonétique*. 4th ed. Paris: Librairie Delagrave.

Hoard, James E. (1978). Syllabication in Northwest Indian languages, with remarks on the nature of syllabic stops and affricates. In Alan Bell and Joan Bybee Hooper (eds.), *Syllables and segments*, 59–72. Amsterdam: North Holland Publishing Company.

Hockett, Charles F. (1955). *A manual of phonology* ( = *Indiana University Publications in Anthropology and Linguistics*, memoir 11). Baltimore: Waverly Press.

Hooper, Joan Bybee (1976). *An introduction to natural generative phonology*. New York: Academic Press.

Hooper, Joan Bybee (1978). Constraints on schwa-delation in American English. In Jacek Fisiak (ed.), *Recent developments in historical phonology,* 183–207. The Hague: Mouton.

Hyman, Larry M. (1985). *A theory of phonological weight*. Dordrecht, Holland: Foris.

Jespersen, Otto (1904). *Lehrbuch der Phonetik*. [4th ed. 1926. Unchanged since 2nd ed. 1912.] Leipzig: B. G. Teubner.

Klingenheben, August (1928). Die Silbenauslautgesetze des Hausa. *Zeitschrift für Eingeborenen-Sprachen* 18.272-297.

Lapesa, Rafael (1965). *Historia de la lengua española*. 6th ed. Madrid: Escelicer.

Leben, William R. (1978). The representation of tone, In Victoria A. Fromkin (ed.), *Tone: A linguistic survey*, 177–219. New York: Academic Press.

Lühr, Rosemarie (1980). Zu einem urgermanischen Lautgesetz. In Manfred Mayrhofer et al. (eds.), *Lautgeschichte und Etymologie: Akten der VI. Fachtagung der Indogermanischen Gesellschaft Wien, 24.–29. September 1978*, 248–259. Wiesbaden: Dr. Ludwig Reichert.

Lutz, Angelika (1985). Die Worttrennung am Zeilenende in altenglischen Handschriften: Phonologische Betrachtungen zu Claus-Dieter Wetzels gleichnamigem Buch. *Indogermanische Forschungen* 90.227-238.

Lutz, Angelika (1986). The syllabic basis of word division in Old English manuscripts. *English Studies* 67.193-210.

Malkiel, Yakov (1968). The inflectional paradigm as an occasional determinant of sound change. In Winfred P. Lehmann and Yakov Malkiel (eds.), *Directions for historical linguistics: A symposium*, 21–64. Austin: University of Texas Press.

Mańczak, Witold (1978). *Fonetica e morfologia storica dell'italiano*. 2nd ed. (= *Uniwersytet Jagielloński, Instytut Filologii Romańskiej, Skrypty Uczelnanie*, 286). Cracow: Nakładem Uniwersytetu Jagiellońskiego.

Mayerthaler, Willi (1982). Markiertheit in der Phonologie. In Theo Vennemann (ed.), *Silben, Segmente, Akzente*, 205–246. Tübingen: Max Niemeyer.

Murray, Robert W. (1982). Consonant developments in Pāli. *Folia Linguistica Historica* 3.163-184.

Murray, Robert W. (1984). *Untersuchungen zur frühgermanischen Silbenstruktur*. Diss. University of Munich. Forthcoming as *Phonological strength and Early Germanic syllable structure* (= *Studies in Theoretical Linguistics*, 6), Munich: Wilhelm Fink.

Murray, Robert W. (1986). Urgermanische Silbenstruktur und die westgermanische Konsonantengemination. *Beiträge zur Geschichte der deutschen Sprache und Literatur* 108.333-356.

Murray, Robert W., and Theo Vennemann (1982). Syllable contact change in Germanic, Greek and Sidamo. *Klagenfurter Beiträge zur Sprachwissenschaft* 8.321-349.

Murray, Robert W., and Theo Vennemann (1983). Sound change and syllable structure [: Problems] in Germanic phonology. *Language* 59.514-528.

Prokosch, Eduard (1939). *A comparative Germanic grammar*. Baltimore: Linguistic Society of America.

# References

Rohlfs, Gerhard (1972). *Historische Grammatik der italienischen Sprache und ihrer Mundarten.* 2nd ed. Vol. 1. Bern: Francke.

de Saussure, Ferdinand (1983). *Cours de linguistique générale: Édition critique préparée par Tullio de Mauro.* Paris: Payot.

Sievers, Eduard (1901). *Grundzüge der Phonetik.* 5th ed. Leipzig: Breitkopf & Härtel.

Sivertsen, Eva (1960). *Cockney phonology* (= *Oslo Studies in English,* 8). Oslo: Oslo University Press.

Streitberg, Wilhelm (1963). *Urgermanische Grammatik.* 3rd ed. Heidelberg: Carl Winter.

Tekavčić, Pavao (1980). *Grammatica storica dell'italiano.* Vol. 1: *Fonematica.* Bologna: Il Mulino.

Varma, Siddheshwar (1961). *Critical studies in the phonetic observations of Indian grammarians.* Delhi: Munshi Ram Manohar Lal. [Reprint of the 1929 edition, London, The Royal Asiatic Society.]

Vennemann, Theo (1978). Universal syllabic phonology. *Theoretical Linguistics* 5.175-215.

Vennemann, Theo (1982). Zur Silbenstruktur der deutschen Standardsprache. In Theo Vennemann (ed.), *Silben, Segmente, Akzente,* 261–305. Tübingen: Max Niemeyer.

Vennemann, Theo (1983a). Causality in language change: Theories of linguistic preferences as a basis for linguistic explanations. *Folia Linguistica Historica* 6.5-26.

Vennemann, Theo (1983b). Überlegungen zu einer Theorie der linguistischen Präferenzen. *Klagenfurter Beiträge zur Sprachwissenschaft* 9.262-292.

Vennemann, Theo (1986). *Neuere Entwicklungen in der Phonologie.* Berlin: Mouton de Gruyter.

Vennemann, Theo (MSa). The rule dependence of syllable structure. Paper presented at the 1984 International Phonology Meeting, Eisenstadt. To appear in *On language: Rhetorica, Phonologica, Syntactica: A festschrift for Robert P. Stockwell from his friends and colleagues,* ed. by Caroline Duncan-Rose et al. Beckenham, Kent: Croom Helm.

Vennemann, Theo (MSb). Syllable cut prosodies in Contemporary Standard German. Paper presented at the 1985 Annual Meeting of the Societas Linguistica Europaea, Toledo.

Vennemann, Theo (MSc). Muta cum Liquida: Worttrennung und Syllabierung im Gotischen: Mit einem Anhang zur Worttrennung in der Pariser Handschrift der althochdeutschen Isidor-Übersetzung. Forthcoming in *Zeitschrift für deutsches Altertum und deutsche Literatur*.

Vincent, Nigel (1973). On gemination in Italian and West Germanic. MS.

Wurzel, Wolfgang Ullrich (1984). *Flexionsmorphologie und Natürlichkeit: Ein Beitrag zur morphologischen Theoriebildung* ( = *Studia Grammatica*, 21). Berlin: Akademie-Verlag.

Zirin, Ronald Andrew (1970). *The phonological basis of Latin prosody*. The Hague: Mouton.

# Index

Page numbers in **boldface** refer to a definition or exemplification. The letter "n." refers to the notes (pages 69–76).

Hock, Hans Henrich
# Principles of Historical Linguistics

1986. XIV, 722 pp. Paperback
ISBN 3110110687
DM 58,—; approx. US $ 33.95

This book provides in up-to-date form an understanding of the Principles of Historical Linguistics and the related fields of comparative linguistics and linguistic reconstruction. In addition, it provides a very broad exemplification for the principles of historical linguistics.

An introductory Chapter 1 is followed by a chapter which provides the necessary background on phonetics, transcription, and related matters. Chapters 3 to 8 deal with sound change, both in its traditional conceptualization by the neogrammarians and in terms of the more recently developed notions of 'contrast' and 'structure and function'. Analogy is discussed in Chapters 9 to 11, the last of these being devoted to the contributions which generative linguistics can make. Chapters 12 and 13 conclude the coverage of 'internal', non-contact induced developments by discussing semantic and syntactic change respectively. Language contact is treated in Chapters 14 to 16. Chapter 14 deals with lexical 'borrowing', 15 covers dialectology, and 16 is devoted to such phenomena as convergence, pidgins, creoles, and language death. Internal reconstruction and comparative linguistics are the topics of Chapters 17 to 19. The last chapter is devoted to a discussion of the general nature and causes of linguistic change.

## Jakobson, Roman, and Waugh, Linda R.
# The Sound Shape of Language

1987. xvi, 335 pp. Paperback
ISBN 3110103982
DM 48,—; approx. US $28.95

This study of the sounds of human languages and their relationship to each other is the last major work by Roman Jakobson, working with Linda R. Waugh. It provides students with a lucid discussion of the many questions which necessarily emerge from an intense involvement with this topic.

Some aspects of speech sounds (distinctive features, phonemes) mean nothing on their own, but are used to differentiate words of different meaning.

Various properties of distinctive features are discussed, including the relation between invariance and variation, synchrony and diachrony, child language acquisition and adult speech, acoustic and articulatory facets, marked and unmarked categories, typology and universals, left and right hemispheres of the brain.

But distinctive features are not the only properties which make up the speech sound: the latter is a complex signal with multiple verbal functions – distinctive, redundant, emotive, configurative, physiognomic.

However, even distinctive features may have some direct connection with meaning. In the last chapter, Jakobson and Waugh investigate the importance of this immediate signaling of meaning in: sound symbolism, mythological transformations of speech, verbal taboo, synesthesia, children's puns, and poetry. They show that the sound shape of language as a whole is endowed with a multitude of signification and that any approach to language must attend to this multiformity.

## Jakobson, Roman, and Halle, Morris
# Fundamentals of Language

1956. 2nd rev. ed. (3rd printing: 1980). 96 pp. Paperback
ISBN 90 279 3074 0
DM 15,—; approx. US $8.95

*Fundamentals of Language* has become a classic in the field of linguistics. It first appeared in 1956, but it is today still of great value, providing as it does a survey of the basic questions of phonology and phonetics in a style accessible to undergraduate students of linguistics.

Almost a quarter of a century separates the publication of *The Sound Shape of Language* from *Fundamentals of Language*, and a quarter of a century before the publication of the latter work, the Prague International Conference established the foundation for general phonology. Thus, the reader of both works can follow the development of work in phonology over 50 years, as presented by one of the great linguists of the century in collaboration, in each case, with one of his students.

## Jakobson, Roman
# Child Language, Aphasia and Phonological Universals

1968. 3rd printing: 1980. 101 pp. Paperback
ISBN 90 279 2103 2
DM 22,—; approx. US $12.95

This work, first published in 1968, made a translation of Jakobson's *Kindersprache, Aphasie und allgemeine Lautgesetze* available to the English speaking world. Although research both in child language acquisition and in aphasia has greatly added to our knowledge in these fields, this short introduction by Jakobson to the many questions in these areas still provides an excellent and stimulating overview.

After a discussion of the phonological development of child language and aphasia as a linguistic problem and the stratification of the phonological system, Jakobson analyses the Foundation of the Structural Laws and indicates prospects for the future.

Linking, as it does, the problems of linguistic universals and of language acquisition, this work will retain its importance in the years to come.

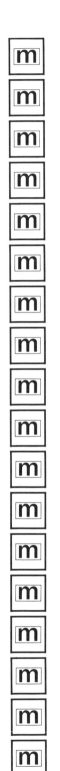

**Fishman, Joshua A.** (Editor)
# Readings in the Sociology of Language

1968. 4th printing: 1977. 808 pp. Paperback
ISBN 90 279 1528 8
DM 49,—; approx. US $28.95

The primary purpose for which these *Readings* have been brought together is to interest students of social behavior in the language determinants, concomitants or consequences of that behavior.

Section I presents a number of papers that may provide the student with greater perspective on the sociology of language as only one of several disciplines viewing language in a behavioral context.

Section II represents an attempt to enter the sociology of language from its more microscopic pole. Here we encounter studies of small group processes, beginning with dyadic encounters and progressing to much longer interactions between somewhat larger face-to-face groups.

Section III presents studies that are concerned with larger categories of mankind (social stratification) and with the within-group and between-group organization (social structure) of these categories.

In Section IV the size of the social groupings under consideration is once more enlarged, this time to the full socio-cultural level. However, in addition, the studies presented were selected from the point of view of reflecting cultural values and socio-cultural change.

Section V is one of two devoted to multilingualism and concentrates on the social, cultural, political and other concomitants of relatively widespread and enduring multilingualism. Section VI is concerned with the circumstances and processes that result in stable or unstable multilingualism. The final section, Section VII, deals with language planning, which is often guided by theoretical considerations and its procedures and outcomes may be productive of new theoretical insights into language-society relationships.

Weinreich, Uriel
# Languages in Contact
## Findings and Problems
1979. xiv, 148 pp. Paperback; ISBN 90 279 2689 1
DM 35,—; approx. US $20.75

This classic considers language contact and bilingualism in the broadest sense, without qualifications as to the degree of difference between the two languages.
After discussing the mechanisms and structural causes of interference, it discusses the bilingual individual. Psychological theories of bilingualism as well as the characteristics of the bilingual speaker and the relative status of the languages are considered. In addition, the speech situation and interference (such factors as stress and specialized uses of language) are examined. There follows an examination of the socio-cultural setting of language contact including such topics as the role of the socio-cultural setting, language functions in bilingual communities, the duration of contact, language shifts, and language loyalty. The study closes with a discussion of research methods and opportunities.

Weinreich, Uriel
# Explorations in Semantic Theory
## With a preface by William Labov
1972. 128 pp. Paperback; ISBN 90 279 2048 6
DM 25,—; approx. US $14.95

The main body of *Explorations* is a formal apparatus for constructing the meaning of a sentence from the meaning of its parts. This formalization is a response to the incentive and challenge provided by Chomsky to rise to a higher level of accountability in formal description. Weinreich's decision to embed his ideas in a formal model based on the current state of generative grammar was a difficult one, since he was well aware that any such machinery was bound to become outmoded.
In any case, Weinreich was obviously not concerned with the survival of the particular concord, transfer, and construal rules which he provides here. In a talk at a conference on computer-related semantic research, he described his own work as "very preliminary and very programmatic" (1965). But by writing rules at a high level of specificity, he demonstrated his confidence that formalization lies at the heart of linguistics, and that further insights depend upon the construction of a formal apparatus with at least this degree of specific accountability.

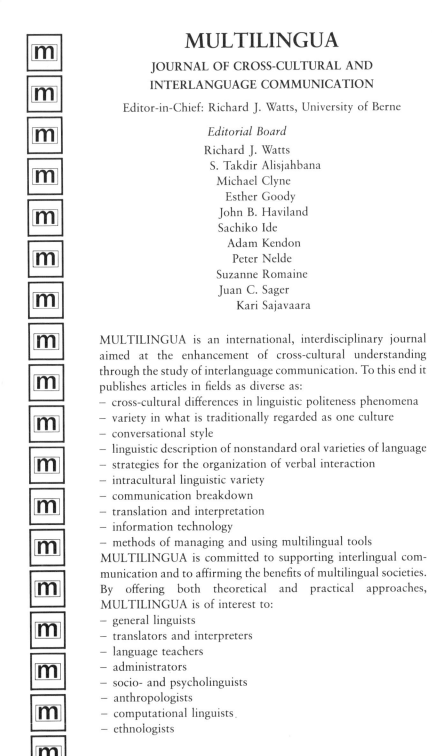

# MULTILINGUA
## JOURNAL OF CROSS-CULTURAL AND INTERLANGUAGE COMMUNICATION

Editor-in-Chief: Richard J. Watts, University of Berne

*Editorial Board*

Richard J. Watts
S. Takdir Alisjahbana
Michael Clyne
Esther Goody
John B. Haviland
Sachiko Ide
Adam Kendon
Peter Nelde
Suzanne Romaine
Juan C. Sager
Kari Sajavaara

MULTILINGUA is an international, interdisciplinary journal aimed at the enhancement of cross-cultural understanding through the study of interlanguage communication. To this end it publishes articles in fields as diverse as:
- cross-cultural differences in linguistic politeness phenomena
- variety in what is traditionally regarded as one culture
- conversational style
- linguistic description of nonstandard oral varieties of language
- strategies for the organization of verbal interaction
- intracultural linguistic variety
- communication breakdown
- translation and interpretation
- information technology
- methods of managing and using multilingual tools

MULTILINGUA is committed to supporting interlingual communication and to affirming the benefits of multilingual societies. By offering both theoretical and practical approaches, MULTILINGUA is of interest to:
- general linguists
- translators and interpreters
- language teachers
- administrators
- socio- and psycholinguists
- anthropologists
- computational linguists
- ethnologists

MULTILINGUA 6-1 (1987), the first issue published under the new editorial program includes the following main articles:

**Richard J. Watts:** Editorial statement

**Joshua A. Fishman:** Post-exilic Jewish languages and pidgin/creoles: Two mutually clarifying perspectives

**Adam Kendon:** Speaking and signing simultaneously in Warlpiri sign-language users

**Dino Bressan:** Emphatic devices in English-Italian translation

MULTILINGUA 7-1/2 (1988) is a special issue devoted to discourse in the nuclear arms debate, edited by James V. Wertsch and Hugh Mehan.

During the past few years scholars from a variety of disciplines have begun to study the discourse of the nuclear arms debate. Their research has examined issues such as patterns of deployment and use of nuclear arms in Japan and the U.S., and the discourse of public relations surrounding superpower summits. In carrying out their studies these scholars have employed ideas from linguistics, semiotics, ethnomethodology, discourse analysis, and other related fields.

MULTILINGUA further publishes research notes, reports, review-articles, short reviews and announcements of upcoming events to keep you up-to-date.

MULTILINGUA will occasionally appear as a special issue, covering a specific topic in one of its fields. The Editor welcomes suggestions for such special issues from its readers.

Contributions for MULTILINGUA should be sent to:

Professor Richard J. Watts

Englisches Seminar

Universität Bern

Gesellschaftsstrasse 6

CH-3012 Bern

Switzerland

MULTILINGUA is published in four issues per volume

Subscription rates for Volume 7 (1988):

| | |
|---|---|
| Institutions | DM 148,—/US $75.00 |
| Individuals (prepaid)* | DM  60,—/US $30.00 |
| Single issue | DM  38,—/approx. US $22.45 |

* The individual rate applies for personal use only and should be ordered directly from the Publishers. The individual rate is not applicable for residents of the FRG, Switzerland or Austria.

# HUMOR

INTERNATIONAL JOURNAL OF HUMOR RESEARCH

Editor-in-Chief: Victor Raskin, Purdue University

This new journal will present a forum for high-quality research on humor as an important and universal human faculty. Having emerged as an interdisciplinary field, humor research draws upon a wide range of academic disciplines including (alphabetically) anthropology, computer science, history, linguistics, literature, mathematics, medicine, philosophy, psychology, and sociology. At the same time, humor research often sheds light on the basic concepts, ideas, and methods of those disciplines.

The journal will publish original contributions including:
– interdisciplinary humor research
– studies on humor theory
– studies of humor research methodologies
– applications of one or more disciplines to the study of humor
– applications of humor research to one or more disciplines
– studies of humor technology
– humor material databases

Contributions will be in the form of empirical, observational studies, theoretical studies, theoretical discussions, presentation of research, short notes, reactions/replies to recent articles, and letters to the editors.

All the materials will be thoroughly refereed.